Succeed at Work Without Sidetracking Your Faith

SUCCEED

AT WORK

WITHOUT SIDETRACKING

YOUR

FAITH

7 LESSONS OF CAREER EXCELLENCE FOR WOMEN

AMY C. BAKER

new
hope
PUBLISHERS

Birmingham, Alabama

New Hope® Publishers
P. O. Box 12065
Birmingham, AL 35202-2065
www.newhopepublishers.com

Library of Congress Cataloging-in-Publication Data

Baker, Amy, 1962-
 Succeed at work without sidetracking your faith : 7 lessons of career excellence for women / Amy Baker.
     p. cm.
 ISBN 1-56309-963-2 (hardcover)
 1. Businesswomen--Religious life. 2. Christian women--Religious life. I. Title.
 BV4596.B8B35 2006
 248.8'8082--dc22

                              2005029001

Produced with the assistance of The Livingstone Corporation (www.LivingstoneCorp.com). Project staff includes Cheryl Dunlop, Linda Taylor, Mary Horner Collins.

ISBN: 1-56309-963-2

N054123 • 0106 • 15M1

*Dedicated, with respect and admiration,
to the modern working woman.*

Table of Contents

Foreword

BY KIM ALEXIS

I became a working woman at age 17, as soon as I graduated high school. My modeling career took off immediately, and I traveled all over the world, appeared on more than 500 magazine covers, and served as a Revlon spokesperson for five years. Yet even in a supposedly "glamorous" career, I faced many challenges that other working women experience. That may come as a surprise to you, but it is true. The biggest challenge I wrestled with was maintaining my integrity when others seemed to think that pushing the envelope was fine. Unfortunately, the boundaries are often hard to see in our world, where people seem to have lost their sense of right and wrong. But I want to encourage you, as a Christian woman in the workplace, to stand as a shining light and a witness for Christ in your sphere of influence.

I encourage you to stand as an example of integrity in the workplace. As working women, I think our biggest challenge is standing up for what is right, even when we think it might hurt our business. I have found that many people in the business world will lie or cheat because they think if they tell the truth, it will cost them money. In the long run, the opposite is true. God honors us when we commit ourselves to integrity in business. God is present with us at work—not only at church or during

Bible study. That divine presence guides us and gives us power to do the right thing, and that is one of the key lessons of *Succeed at Work Without Sidetracking Your Faith*.

GOD AND THE MODELING WORLD

Integrating our faith into our work lives requires most of us to maintain a delicate balance. Let me tell you what I mean. I became a Christian in 1990. I had grown up going to church but didn't really understand what a personal relationship with God was like until I was well into adulthood and struggling in a failing marriage. I soon recognized that in the modeling world, as I became more and more outspoken for God, my jobs began to decline. When others were willing to compromise themselves in a photo shoot and I refused to do something, I was often made to feel like a stuffed shirt. There were times I literally felt sick to my stomach and realized it was because I was being pushed into something I felt was wrong. I would have to talk to the client about it. Sometimes they understood, other times they didn't and I lost the business.

Don't get me wrong—there were many aspects of my very public career that were fascinating. One was the travel. I enjoyed meeting many people who were different from me, leading very different lives in different cultures and countries. My job gave me the opportunity to experience the diversity of God's creation. I was taken out of the "bubble" of my own little world. As a working woman, you probably also meet many people you wouldn't otherwise meet. Christian working women have a unique opportunity to impact the world for

Christ because often our sphere of influence is broader. We get out of our neighborhoods and have the chance to interact with others who are hurting and need a smile or a kind word. Sharing our faith is sometimes that simple.

YOUR PLACE OF INFLUENCE

I have learned, and am continuing to learn, the balance required to integrate my faith and work. I am learning to be outspoken when asked about my beliefs, but not pushy. I wait for the opportunity to speak the truth. The rest of the time, I try to set an example of what it means to have a relationship with Jesus. Sometimes it is easy to share our faith, but hard to know when the timing is right. Fortunately, if we ask Him, God gives us wisdom to speak a word of encouragement or hope at the right time. He will also guide us to understand that *how* we do our work speaks much more than mere words about our relationship with God.

As my career has changed and I have grown closer to the Lord, my perspective on work has changed. It might surprise you to know that I do not think of myself as famous or great. Sure, it is nice to see yourself on the cover of a magazine, but all those magazine covers will be forgotten some day. I have been humbled to realize that all I have has been given to me for a purpose, and that purpose is to *help* others, not make other women feel inferior or ugly. You may never be on the cover of a magazine, but that doesn't mean you don't have impact on the lives of the people you work with.

Not all our jobs are glamorous or glitzy in the eyes of the world. You might feel like you are not working up to your potential, or you may currently be in a job that does not thrill you. God can still use you; you can still fulfill a higher purpose. There are many things I do that I do not want to do now that my career has changed, but I count it joy to work for God because I know that He has a purpose and plan for me—He has had that plan all along. Even when I wasn't paying attention!

All women in the work world—regardless of what we do—have the opportunity to make a difference. It was once said that if we do not stand up for what is right and good, then sooner or later others will not know what good is. We are to be a shining light for God in the office, at the grocery store, the auto mechanic or at our kids' school—wherever we are.

Will I struggle with difficult career situations? Sure. Will there be conflicts and difficult choices? Of course. Those tough circumstances happen to all of us at one time or another during our working lives. What I know though, is that God is watching over us. When we are willing to learn and grow, God uses those rough times for good in our lives. To get to that place of personal and spiritual learning and growth, we have to change our attitudes about work and why we work. Suddenly, it isn't all about us anymore. It is about what we can give, not what we can get. In this book, Amy Baker makes this point very clear. It is a lesson every working woman should take to heart.

AN INSPIRING WOMAN

What do I want people to remember about Kim Alexis? My answer to that question has changed over the years. Today I would say that I don't want people to remember that I was a model and that my face was on magazine covers. I want people to remember that I was inspiring. I want women to realize that in Christ, we are *overcomers* and I want my life to demonstrate that.

I bet you don't want to be remembered for being the best accountant, or best manager, or best store clerk. Sure, those things are important—of course we want to do our best, but what's most important is realizing that we make a difference in people's lives. As you consider your career, I encourage you to ask God what He would have you do for Him each day. God desires, and has the power, to align us and position us to be where we are for *His* purposes. Let God surprise you with His direction and His love. When you lean on Him, and lean into the plan He has for you, you will see that you can succeed at work, and not sidetrack, but actually grow in your faith.

Acknowledgments

I want to thank everyone I've ever worked for. Seriously, I have had remarkable managers throughout my career. From each of you I learned about myself, my skills, my potential, and even my limitations.

While my other career positions at The University of Texas, Texans' War on Drugs, and the Texas Apartment Association were significant milestones in my professional life, nothing can compare to eleven years, eleven months, and fifteen or so days at Dell. It is indisputably one of the most intriguing stories of entrepreneurship and competitive valor in the history of corporate America. I literally would not be writing this book had I not experienced what I did at that company.

While those folks I worked with are certainly significant, the amazing people I live with are even more so. My husband never begrudged a late-night meeting or overnight business trip. He has always been my greatest supporter and biggest fan, and he continues to encourage me to press beyond the boundaries of my own imagination (and sometimes skills). Wayne, thank you. You're my one and only.

To my children, Charlie and Karen. Thank you for your prayers that my books would be published, for believing in your mom and for being happy with frozen pizza when deadlines loomed. You are the greatest kids in the world! You make your momma proud.

As I wrote and researched, my intercessory team was just at the other end of email, and they were steadfast in their prayers and encouragement. Thanks, friends.

Neither of my recently published books would have come to fruition had it not been for the amazing ministry of Florence and Marita Littauer and CLASServices. Their knowledge of this business and heart for God is a huge inspiration to countless wannabe authors and speakers. Marita especially deserves many thanks and lots of hugs for recognizing the distinct need for a book like this and pushing me to go for it.

God has opened doors for me throughout my life that I could never have envisioned. From national TV news appearances to meeting First Lady Nancy Reagan to writing speeches for a CEO, the opportunities for success, satisfaction, and significance have been amazing. I have made my share of mistakes and had more than a few career mishaps, but God has always worked it out for my good. What's more, He has kept me in the palm of His hand and, in spite of my veering to the left or right occasionally, He helped keep my own faith from being sidetracked throughout the roller-coaster ride we all experience as working women.

Thank You to my Heavenly Father for giving me one more opportunity to use the gifts He has given me to advance His glory. He is the one true source of all success, satisfaction, and significance.

Amy C. Baker

Introduction

I was sipping my coffee and applying the usual potions to ward off wrinkles when I heard an intriguing research report on the morning news. "U.S. job satisfaction keeps falling, the Conference Board reports today."

No big surprise there. As a human resources executive, I ran more employee opinion surveys than I care to remember. Those years of working with employees taught me that many people, regardless of position or role, often felt a nagging dissatisfaction with their work, or manager, or company, or all three. The causes varied, but often when we dug around in the data, we would find that the employee was not planning for their own career development. They wanted HR to *fix* their careers. But no matter how much I might have wanted to, I could not sprinkle pixie dust on someone and transform them into a rising-star employee overnight.

In the last 30 or 40 years, working Americans observed a fascinating but scary transition: the dissolution of the employment relationship as it had always been defined. Here's a perfect example. My father worked for the same company for 46 years. He moved slowly and methodically up the corporate ladder, settling comfortably into mid-management, where he stayed contentedly until retiring at age 71! He faithfully did his job, his company took care of him, and his pension and health benefits were more than sufficient to care for him and my mom until they passed away.

In today's corporate culture, we see this scenario only rarely. Neither companies nor employees assume the permanence of a job. We job shop—we are free agents moving where the spirit leads or the wind blows looking for that next great opportunity. We no longer have a clear-cut path laid out for us—we have to forge our own paths. In this quick-change atmosphere, it's no wonder more and more employees are feeling dissatisfied at work!

But here's my challenge to you: If that is true, then what are you going to *do* about it? Are you ready to take charge of your own career planning? If you do, you can create a career that not only leads you to success, but also to more personal satisfaction and fulfillment of your vocational calling in God's Kingdom. Using your God-given gifts, applying divinely inspired attitudes, and approaching work from a much bigger perspective, you *can* have an impact on three very important things:

- How successful you are
- How satisfied you are with your working life
- How significant an impact you have on the world around you

OWN YOUR CAREER

If you agree with the presupposition that we own our careers, then this book is for you. Perhaps you are just starting out, graduating from college or a vocational training program and about to launch a new career. Maybe you have been in the workplace a while and are thinking about making a change or wondering how to get ahead. Or you may be ready to re-enter the work-force after a time at home with the kids.

Whatever your current place in the ever-changing world of work, this book holds a treasure or two for you. In it we go through several key lessons about work in the world today.

• We will talk about behaviors and action plans that help us achieve a higher level of **excellence at work** and keep our faith from getting sidetracked in the process.

• We will hear **stories and advice from other women** in the workplace who have learned to pursue their careers and grow in their faith at the same time—women who have an impact for the Kingdom regardless of their role or title.

• We will **broaden our view of success** beyond what the world defines.

• We will consider ways to **find satisfaction** in our work life even when we might not be in our dream job.

• We will explore the **significant contribution** we can make to God's kingdom work—showing His love to a love-starved world—regardless of our position, title, or employer.

• We will also see the **biblical principles** embedded throughout effective career practices—confirmation that it is possible to be ambitious, have job-related aspirations, and be committed to our faith at the same time.

Each chapter concludes with homework—both things for you to think about and things for you to do. This book lends itself to not only personal study but small group discussion as well. Perhaps you'll find a handful of other women at work, in your neighbor-hood, or at church with whom you can explore these concepts and grow together. There's no hidden camera to make sure you do this, but I promise you will see more progress if you put extra effort in the game.

THE CHARACTERISTICS OF EXCELLENCE

When I was in my late 30s, I began to explore the research surrounding career development and successful leadership. I also helped develop numerous training and development programs throughout my career and saw firsthand what worked and what didn't. When I began to understand the characteristics that led to success, I realized that much of my own experience taught me clearly what makes people more successful. I also discovered that by luck, grace, good genes, or street smarts, much of my behavior at work and in my personal adventures—*how I worked at work*—contributed to me being a more successful and valuable employee and team member.

Certainly there were setbacks and heartaches. But by recounting some of the brick walls I ran into myself, I hope to help you avoid them, or at least just bump into them with only minor injury!

What follows are some of the most important lessons I learned. They are things I wish someone had told me when I was 22, as I was bursting forth into the world with a college diploma and dreams of success. Who knows? I just might have listened.

This isn't just another "self-help" job book based on a bunch of fancy research by highly paid consultants. It's not rocket science or brain surgery. It contains practical suggestions from a very down-to-earth and direct person who's coached everyone from mail-room clerks to corporate executives.

It's also the perspective of someone who's had to sit across the desk from colleagues at all those levels to tell them they no longer had a job. And that unfortunate outcome usually wasn't the result of their functional or technical skills or what they did. The devastating event was all too often because of *how they did it*.

You don't want to settle for mediocrity. To survive and thrive in today's chaotic business environment, only personal and professional excellence will do. This book is for anyone who wants to excel at what they do. Although it is written from the context of working in a paid job, the principles apply if you are looking for a job, running a home, volunteering at the homeless shelter, or considering an entry into the marketplace.

Let's launch now into this discussion of succeeding at work without sidetracking your faith. Let's study together these seven lessons that can lead to both career excellence and exciting change and growth. The fundamental principles in this book are designed to challenge your assumptions, propel you toward new behavior, get you to look at your current patterns of thought, and bring about changes that can contribute to a professional life filled with excellence, impact, and personal spiritual growth. So let's do it, women! As women of faith in the marketplace, we can work excellently and love God deeply at the same time. "With Him, all things are possible."

CHAPTER ONE

Your Career— Your Choice

LESSON #1
CAREER PLANNING IS YOUR JOB—EVEN IF IT'S NOT ON YOUR JOB DESCRIPTION.

"Great ability develops and reveals itself increasingly with every new assignment."
—Baltasar Gracian

Where are you? I don't mean sitting on the back porch or on the bus or in an airplane. I mean, where are you in your career?

Just starting out? Graduating from college with a freshly minted diploma, a heart full of dreams, and a stomach full of butterflies? Wondering if anything you learned in your internship or practicum will actually apply in the real world?

Maybe you have a job and don't know what to do with it. Are you parked in neutral and just hanging out waiting for something to happen, or are you ready to move around within your existing organization?

Perhaps you are ready to make a big leap. You've been thinking for a while that the grass looks greener somewhere else, but you are not sure how to approach a career change.

Or maybe it is time to go back into the workforce. You have taken time off to raise your kids and now that they're older you need a break from the shopping channel and food network. Ready to go back to that career you put on hold or discover a new one?

These are just a few of the questions women ask when it comes to owning and planning their careers. Maybe you are thinking, *Career? How is selling cosmetics at the department store a career?* Whatever you do, you can do it excellently, with purpose, and in a fashion to lead to personal and spiritual growth and development.

Growing professionally is much like growing spiritually. To grow deeply in love with our Lord, we don't just show up at church. We invest time in His Word and in worship, fellowship, and prayer. To grow in our jobs, we don't just show up on Monday morning. We need a strategy to continue honing our skills and abilities regardless of what they are.

These concepts are true even if you have your sights set on a window office in the headquarters building, or are content in your current position. You may be a clerk at the corner drugstore or filling boxes in an inventory warehouse, perfectly happy to do your job and go home at the end of the day with little thought of work until eight or nine the next morning. You can still strive to do those jobs, no matter how unglamorous, with excellence and enthusiasm that befits a daughter of the King!

Jobs are defined very differently nowadays. Our society, and the job market, experiences changes that often occur at lightning speed, requiring us to think differently about long-term career planning.

The Bible has lots to say about work. It tells us that we are each hard-wired with certain gifts and abilities, and they apply not just to what church committee we serve on, but also what we do from eight to five.

JOB OR WORK?

In his book *Creating You & Co.,* William Bridges suggests that the concept of a job is different now. In fact, "jobs" in the traditional sense don't exist. What needs to be done is *work*. His recommendation to manage our careers is to "find work that needs doing, and present yourself to whoever needs it as the best way to get it done." With this perspective, we not only increase the likelihood of meaningful and stable employment, but we are constantly learning in the process.

These lessons apply to us regardless of our position or company. When I was a college kid working in a gift shop, I saw the way the part-time clerks operated. Some looked for extra things to do and some did just what was required to get by. Go-getters noticed the shelf that needed dusting and the register tape that needed reordering every six weeks, and they were the ones who got the hefty quarter-an-hour-raises. They were the ones who worked their way into greater responsibility and became gift buyers and inventory managers. It was an early lesson in creating one's own job and owning one's own plan, even at a seemingly menial level.

Let me share with you how this has played out in my own life. I have had a remarkably diverse career. When you look at the résumé, you see that it has taken me across the map from an industry standpoint.

- Worked in a retail gift shop throughout college
- Spent two summers at a Christian camp: first year as counselor, second as program director
- Worked at a state government job for a big university after graduation from a small university
- Transitioned to a nonprofit with a federally-funded (read cheap) budget
- Moved to a real-estate-related association where I ran communications and marketing
- Rocketed into high-tech corporate America at the beginning of the booming 1990s and spent nearly 12 years at Dell, Inc., a company that went from 1,500 to nearly 40,000 employees during my tenure
- Started my own business-consulting practice and became a sole practitioner in a market full of people doing similar things

Sure, there are common threads throughout all those positions. They all required communications skills, people skills, and good project management, but the similarity ends there. They were very different roles. Tasks included a wide range of responsibilities and skills.

- Training college students to sell newspaper ads and present themselves professionally even after pulling an all-nighter studying for an exam
- Helping mobilize young people and communities against drug abuse during the height of the *Just Say No* era
- Marketing and communications for a real-estate professionals' association, where I learned more about rental property than I ever really cared to know
- Human resources leadership and internal communications management for a dynamic high-tech company
- Using my communication skills in a variety of situations to help small businesses and individuals achieve their competitive goals, while also ministering to people through my writing and speaking

I consider myself very fortunate to have worked in spectacularly different industries. Not all my job changes represented a significant increase in pay or a bump to a more glamorous title. But they were all *different*. And the managers I worked for and teams I participated in were also very *different*.

Skills I had learned in previous jobs applied to the next one, but I sometimes had to figure out how those skills translated. I mentioned common themes:

communications, people, and project management. It appeared that no matter what positions I held, these skills and experiences were called upon.

DISCOVER YOUR STRENGTHS

It's a theme played out in the book *Now, Discover Your Strengths*, based on research by The Gallup Organization. In it, authors Marcus Buckingham and Donald O. Clifton help us understand our own talents and strengths and how to capitalize on them. Once we're clear on what those are, we build our career paths around what we are good at instead of basing our path on our weaknesses, as is so often the case. It should be "You're great at this—do it more!" instead of "You're not good at this—fix it. This is not an excuse to ignore our weaknesses, but a reminder to use our strengths to attack those areas we need to improve.

Jesus built His ministry this way. He turned a group of fishermen into fishers of men who learned His message and taught it to others. He turned a tent maker into the greatest church planter the world has ever known. After meeting Jesus, a zealous tax collector began to use his powers of persuasion and political connections for something much more significant. The list goes on and on. Jesus tapped marketplace leaders like Zaccheus to rock the world. Our God-ordained gifts and talents were meant to be used not just on church committees but in the workplace, where we spend our days.

Managing a career path is not always about moving up. It can be about moving around and within a business or industry to gain meaningful experience that makes us more valuable to our employers, gives us pride in our accomplishments, and uses our strengths and talents so we can compensate for areas where we are weaker. It is about looking for opportunities where we can affect the kingdom of God and not just make a living, but make a life.

MEET DEE ANN TURNER

Dee Ann Turner is the vice president of human resources for Chick-Fil-A, Inc., in Atlanta. She has built a very successful career on a similar philosophy. "Long ago I was encouraged to win people over with my competencies and not pay attention to anything else." This approach obviously worked, because Dee Ann started out with Chick-Fil-A in 1985 as an administrator. She was a preacher's wife who never expected to become a corporate VP, but God had that in mind for her.

Dee Ann says, "At some point in my career I realized that because of my relationship with God and my desire to commit my work to Him, the outcome had already been planned. It was just up to me to use my strengths and follow His path, figuring out what I was supposed to do and then letting God direct me. Work became more about calling than career." As a human resources professional, she coaches employees with this same advice. It is advice gleaned not from a workshop or seminar but based on her real life experience.

Dee Ann is one of many successful women from all walks of life who have found that it is possible to integrate work into our life's calling and our giftedness. She also knows the value of trusting the Lord with our jobs but still having a plan. "I tell people all the time that this is a do-it-yourself world. We cannot depend on others to write us a prescription for our jobs. Depending on God, though, works *really* well!"

When I was a human resources executive, some of the most painful conversations I had with people surrounded the direction of their career path. The long-held perception is that "up is the only way to go." Self-image and mortgage payments become closely tied to the idea that each subsequent career move should reflect a more important title and higher salary. The primary image that comes to mind when we talk about career path is a ladder, and it is not lying on its side, it's heading up.

Well, the old trusty career ladder ain't what it used to be.

First, most organizations are shaped like a funnel and, unfortunately, the top is the narrow end. The assumption is that up top is where all the money, prestige, and power lies, and that "top" always has the title "management" attached to it. But nowadays, the shift to virtual teams, just-in-time workforces, and consultants for project management makes the funnel even narrower and the career ladder even more rickety.

The second problem with this "up is the only way to go" perception is that it is like looking at our careers with tunnel vision. Our sight becomes narrow. We do the same thing, day after day, with only slight increases in scope and responsibility, and our careers come to an end someday with little true personal growth or development. We may have moved from widget maker I to widget maker II to widget maker III, but all we did was make widgets. Or perhaps we moved into widget making manager and moved up that food chain, but did we grow much in the process? Did we really experience all God had for us and have the greatest possible impact for Him from eight to five?

Read carefully, friend. It may sound like I'm contradicting myself, but I'm not. Movement isn't always about "up," but it is about progress—focusing on getting better and having greater impact regardless of the weight of our title or size of our salary.

OWN YOUR CAREER

What does it mean for us to own our career path? How do we think about career ambition in light of the Bible's exhortation to be humble and "not to think of ourselves more highly than we should"? What do we learn from men like my father?

I believe it is a lesson about operating in our giftedness and in God's timing. It is also about the biblical principle of making a plan. Here is how that has played out for me. See if you see similar patterns in your career and how you spend your leisure time.

I am a communicator. I tell stories. I connect with people through conversation and presentations and writing. Don't even think about asking me to manage a spreadsheet or analyze a budget. I'd wither up and die and get it all wrong in the end. I've wanted to write books for as long as I can remember, but God didn't open those doors until just recently. I needed to cross a few bridges and trudge a few hard roads to prepare me for this (and believe me, there are days when I think I'm still not prepared).

My husband is gifted in areas of mercy and intuition and insight. He has a level of compassion and empathy for people that I only dream about having. He used to kid me that when distraught employees came into my office for help I would only give them *one* Kleenex.

My terrific spouse is in the midst of his mid-life career change now too, becoming a licensed professional counselor. God has given him the life experiences of husband, father, successful businessman, and school-teacher to position him to be highly effective now as a marriage and family therapist. Although he wanted to go this route when we were first mar-

MOVEMENT ISN'T ALWAYS ABOUT "UP," BUT IT IS ABOUT PROGRESS.

ried, the timing was not right. Now with almost twenty (yikes!) years of marriage behind us, a successful career in high tech to his credit, a stint teaching middle school math, and the experience of parenting two dramatically different kids, God has opened the doors for him to move down this new path. In both my example and my husband's, we are doing what we love, using our divinely ordained gifts and walking down roads God has opened for us in His timing, not ours.

Alexander Graham Bell said, "When one door closes another door opens; but we often look so long and so regretfully upon the closed door, that we do not see the ones which open for us." This is an important lesson for career management because it puts the focus on God's will, purpose, and timing for our lives, not goals based solely on the world's definition of success.

When it comes to our jobs, most of us have an ideal plan—the career to make a life—our dream job. Most of us also have to make a living—we need a job to pay the bills. At times, we may find ourselves accomplishing less than we'd like and doing something we don't really enjoy, but at the same time we are learning important life lessons that may enable us to eventually launch on the path to what our heart has always called us to do.

THE BIBLE ON CAREER PLANNING

There's plenty in Scripture about planning, by the way, and it's not a stretch to think of those verses in terms of our career. For one, there is Proverbs 16:3, "Commit to the LORD whatever you do, and your plans will succeed." Hand in hand with that though, we see the wisdom in Proverbs 16:9, "In his heart a man plans his course, but the LORD determines his steps." Our plans, be they for our career, who we marry, or what state we live in, are determined by our heavenly Father who loves us beyond words. He promises us success when we commit those plans to Him. And most of us know from experience that His view of success doesn't always mirror ours! Neither is His timing necessarily synchronized to our quickly ticking quartz watches.

Isn't it interesting that Jesus didn't start His earthly ministry until he was thirty? Moses didn't launch the "let my people go" campaign until he was well into his eighties. Abraham and Sarah didn't become parents until way past the time their maternity coverage had expired. Paul had a successful tent-making company before he began to write a large chunk of the New Testament. Then there were all those fishermen who found themselves casting for a very different catch after their encounter with Jesus.

We learn from these wise words, ancient stories, and present day examples that the God-defined seasons of our lives aren't always in sync with our calendars. His timing operates in a different warp, but we are assured in Psalm 139 that He ordained all our days. The steps toward our dream career path—toward fulfilling our calling—may be circuitous and full of detours, but when we are set on using the talents He's given us, when we seek His counsel to make a plan, He will give us the desires of our heart, especially when our aim is to glorify Him.

Furthermore, when we're using the talents He's given us and consciously committing our ways to Him, we're less likely to fall into the trap of vain and arrogant ambition. "It's hard to be humble when…" —you fill in the blank. We live in a culture saturated with self-esteem training and even go to churches where false humility is just that—a cover-up for our pride and just how much we know about the Bible. However, when we're focused on our hearts—the core of our being, where the Lord has gifted us and called us to serve—we find ourselves working with confidence, succeeding without having to walk on others' backs, and generally having a good time doing it.

How does this apply in real life and real work? First, we do well to remember that management isn't the only way to go. Organizations constantly make people-management decisions that ultimately fail. The best salesperson gets promoted to sales management. The most brilliant engineer leaps to engineering manager. The outrageously creative genius is put in charge of the art department. And then things fall apart.

The skills that make those people great individual contributors don't always transfer well when they are asked to shepherd a group of people who often have the same skills and personality they do. We can avoid career heartbreak by not letting ourselves get swept into a path that leads us into a role we are not suited for.

For the individual who works in a small company or is self-employed, the career challenge is the same; the decision-making path just looks different. People with a reputation for getting the job done often get asked to do more and more. But that more and more may not necessarily be in sync with their skills and abilities. In that case, that person may want to ensure that the management team knows what their top skills are. Using those specific skills, not adding projects that cause them to underachieve or fail, can solve business problems.

WHAT ABOUT SELF-EMPLOYMENT?

Self-employment presents a unique set of issues. The issue is not about managing a "career path," so to speak, but rather managing the business's growth and one's professional development. I've heard other independent consultants discuss the difficult decision to turn away work that doesn't fit their fundamental skill set. There might be good money to be made, but the self-employed must ask themselves if it is worth the risk to their reputation to deliver a substandard product or service.

Instead, successful independent business professionals must focus their marketing to highlight their talents and target potential clients where they know they can add value and deliver the goods. They are still growing and learning because they are producing something different for each client, facing a different set of business challenges each time, but they are not necessarily set on the bigger-client-is-always-better path.

AN IMPACT FOR GOD

You don't always have to be the one in the spotlight to be significant. Moses had Aaron. Paul had Timothy. Esther had Mordecai. The Bible is full of stories of individuals who didn't have leadership positions, fancy titles, and corner offices, but still impacted their nations, encouraged their mentors, and saved their people through the scope of their influence. Career planning in the twenty-first century employs the same principles: The best way is to use your God-given talents, in God's given time, with a focus on His glory and goals. Learning and personal growth are accomplished by doing new things, seeking new challenges, and even inventing new job descriptions, all with an eye toward the Kingdom.

Look at Paul's words in 2 Corinthians 8:7, "But just as you excel in everything—in faith, in speech, in knowledge, in complete earnestness and in your love for us—see to it that you also excel in this grace of giving." We strive for excellence in all things—and when our ultimate aim is to give of ourselves, that's true success, success that has not sidetracked but rather grown our faith.

PLANNING YOUR CAREER

So you have a job and, generally, you like what you do. A move outside your company is not on your radar screen (and as far as you know, not on your manager's either!). You can still take some initiative to own your long-term plan and your professional development. When doing this work on your career path, consider not just titles, money, and prestige. Instead think about:

- The work that needs to be done to meet your organization's goals
- The results that can be delivered to the advantage of your team and company
- The stated or unstated skills that your business values and hires
- The characteristics of successful leaders inside your business
- Growth opportunities for you and your team if you're a manager
- Skill builders to capitalize on your strengths and make up for your weaknesses
- Areas for development and growth—where you are weak
- Whom you can learn from—who models success

These are the considerations that lead to a path of best results when it comes to our careers.

Does it seem overwhelming? It might if you've never thought about it all before. The great news is this: A multitude of resources are available to help you land on that right path when you make the commitment to your own development. If you have the time and resources, look for qualified and well-regarded career coaches in your area. There is also a variety of information on the Web, and many self-assessments tools that are free or inexpensive.

It is also important to get *objective* data about your strengths and weaknesses, your skills and abilities. If you have kept any performance reviews you have received throughout your career, pull them out and look for trends. If your organization offers 360-degree assessments, where peers, subordinates, and managers rate your competencies, take advantage of that if you can. Our own opinions of ourselves tend to be a bit lopsided!

In the rest of the book you are going to learn strategies that will help you develop professionally: developing political savvy, learning excellent customer service skills, overcoming hang-ups around job titles, understanding the value of mentoring and importance of integrity. These are just a few of the things that can help you be more successful regardless of your position or company. Blending the career management skills with these critical competencies is crucial to owning your own career development.

Although we are very interested in managing and owning our careers, there is also another goal of this book, in fact the most important goal of all: to reflect the love of God in the workplace.

MEET LUCI SWINDOLL

Luci Swindoll knows a thing or two about this concept. She is the show-stopping speaker for Women of Faith conferences. Prior to that role, Luci had a successful 30-year career with Mobil Oil, rising to the executive ranks in a field dominated by men. Then she joined Insight for Living as vice president of public relations. Today, she headlines conferences that reach the souls of women from all walks of life with heart-level inspiration and slumber-party-like fun.

She recalls women she knew who would spend the night in the office bathroom just to be the first one there in the morning. "There is nothing wrong with being driven,"

Luci says. "We are all driven by something, but when our greatest passion becomes making money and being successful, we are headed down the wrong path and we become unapproachable. When that happens, we can't fulfill our highest calling, which is to be Christ in the workplace—that is our number one priority."

Some people aim low, in order to reach their goals and avoid disappointment. Others are so fixated on title and money and fame that they burn out, leave a path of wounded co-workers in their wake, and never go home happy at the end of the day. The key to being on the path with the most results is finding the right path to begin with, one that capitalizes on our God-given talents. We must sincerely seek what He has called us to do. Timing is everything. Most of us trudge through a few less-than-idyllic jobs or companies before we land in the career of our dreams, and that's okay!

So what if you're ready to make a move?

"I'M READY TO BAIL OUT!"

Perhaps you've already jumped, or, as is often the case, been pushed from the plane at 10,000 feet with minimal instruction and a parachute you've never used. You are job hunting seriously and trying to figure out how to land safely in the job market jungle. It's time for some serious inspection of your resources and a new map.

Here is part of a well-thought-out plan from John McDorman, a career transition expert and outplacement provider. He developed a Career Transition Workshop that is used in churches throughout the country. He calls the first step in the journey to a new job "accepting the axe." Having spent a few years in employee relations and having managed layoffs and downsizings, I couldn't agree more that this is a critical step. Whether your exit from a job was voluntary or involuntary, there are chapters that need to be closed before you can successfully launch a new job search.

Even when our departure was our idea, we still carry out a bit of baggage with our personal effects when we turn in our badge and leave the office or warehouse for the last time. There was that missed promotion or embarrassing situation in an operations review last quarter. A relationship with a co-worker went south and never came back. The cute girl in accounting got a lateral position you'd applied for, and it still hurt when you saw her at the coffee bar.

When we leave a job for the last time, it is time to leave that stuff at the door. Luci Swindoll, in her book *Notes to a Working Woman*, reminds women that "nothing is ever wasted in God's economy." When it comes to transitions in the workplace Luci advises us to "drop those bags in the middle of the road and keep walking." The insults we remember, the situations that still turn our cheeks red and make our hearts pound have likely been forgotten by everyone else. Now it is our turn.

This is my most often repeated piece of advice for those who have been hurt at work—*truth will prevail.* When the office politics have lined up against you and the least deserving have gotten the most, you desire justice at any cost. Many times, though, the cost isn't worth it and it is best to let justice take its course in due time.

Leaving a job with our bridges intact, not burned by our own defensiveness or bitterness, is one of the best ways to move into a new career search with a positive outlook and assurance that we did what we could to make things right. Sometimes, this means going to a co-worker and asking for forgiveness when we have not handled a past conflict the way we should have. Usually, folks respond with overwhelming gratitude, surprise, and an apology you never expected to hear.

To show you an example, let's go back to the cutie at the coffee bar. You were both vying for the same job in your department. Not a step up, but a better slot on the ladder's rung, and even though you had more experience, and you *thought* a better track record, she got the job. From then on, interactions at the copy machine or coffee pot were stiff at best. You never actually threw paper clips into her cubicle, but you sure thought about it, and she avoided you.

LEAVING A JOB WITH YOUR BRIDGES INTACT IS ONE OF THE BEST WAYS TO MOVE AHEAD.

Here's what I mean by rebuilding those bridges as you leave behind a company and the inevitable conflicts that arose there: "Hey Sally, you got a minute? You know it's my last day, and I wanted to apologize for treating you unkindly after you got the job we both wanted. It was not right for me to snub you, and I'm sorry. I wish you the best here."

Gulp.

You *can* do this. It may take a week of prayer on your weak knees and all the power of the Holy Spirit, but think what is accomplished. You not only leave your old company with a clean conscience, but you show a bit of God's grace and forgiveness to a co-worker who may never see that kind of love again.

This fictional scenario gets even better if she apologizes too and then asks how in the world you had the guts to approach her. "Well, let me tell you about a Man I know who gives me the power to do just about anything..."

That's the micro-perspective of accepting the axe and moving on from a job and company you are leaving. What about the macro-perspective? That's the 20,000-foot view of the company and managers you are leaving behind—the view from 20,000 feet in the air.

Let's say things never quite worked out the way you'd planned there. The promises of the recruiting team and your original hiring manager never quite came to fruition. In fact, your hiring manager disappeared three reorganizations ago. Whether you leave because you are forced out or laid off or outsourced, your disdain toward the company and the people who run it can be substantial if you are not careful.

At this point it is important to remember two fundamental premises of business: One, businesses are comprised of fallible people who make mistakes, just like you and me; and two, at the end of the day or quarter or annual report, business is mostly about profit.

Sometimes, a management team must make incredibly difficult decisions that affect people in a significant way because of the bottom line. Even companies that are committed to employee satisfaction, even those that realize profits can be driven through great people management, will still have to make tough choices. We may not like it, but that's the way it is.

I do not advocate getting a poster board and parading up and down the parking lot with a sign that reads,

"I forgive you, you shmucks!" The issue is an attitude adjustment. Remember the big picture, try not to take it personally, and move on.

The next step in moving on is beginning to focus on our future. Any change is the opportunity for a new adventure. It's a chance for God to surprise us.

My son Charlie learned this for the first time two years ago. His sixth-grade year at school was blissful. Academically, he worked hard but didn't have to knock himself out to make good grades. He had two best buddies: Steven, a guy he'd known since preschool, and his friend Emily, probably his first real crush (although they never admitted to that). On the flip side, he also had strained relationships with some of his other guy friends—the result of raging hormones and growing egos. As May rolled around, dark clouds loomed on the horizon.

In addition to the stress of entering seventh grade and middle school, with new levels of accountability and responsibility, Charlie learned that Emily and Steven were not coming back. Steven was moving to a new school and Emily's family was moving to a new town with her dad's job. Charlie was heartbroken and very despondent.

"I don't even want to go back to school next fall. Why don't you just home-school me?" he asked. He was blue all summer as he spent as much time as he could with these friends before the demands of seventh grade and a moving truck pulled them apart. In August, I really began to encourage him and we earnestly began to pray.

"Charlie," I kept saying, "Leave room for God to surprise you." After the first day of seventh grade, it was clear that our gracious Lord had done just that for this young man wrestling with the emotional throes of adolescence. "I had a great day, Mom!" He started rattling off who he'd lunched with and his plans for football practice. A new day had dawned in his school career.

LET GOD SURPRISE YOU

A job change for us can mark the dawn of a new day for our careers and a chance for God to surprise us as well. I talked to countless people both during and after one company's big layoff who said, "In the end, it was the best thing that could have happened."

Jan Shurtz is a consultant in Chicago. She provides career transition coaching, leadership, and team development to individuals and businesses. Her goal is to help people find jobs faster and more effectively, and when in a new job, to find continued success and satisfaction at work. Two of her top career transition tips are, first, maintain a positive attitude and be careful not to concentrate on bad business or economic news. Second, she advises that you communicate your targeted career focus and weekly goals to your spouse or close friends. Jan says, "The job search can be isolating and lonely. Keeping those close to you up to date on your progress connects you to others." An added bonus? Well, according to Jan, those folks you've kept up to date throughout your transition can then celebrate with you as you reach your milestones.

God brings hope to the despairing and works out all the wacky circumstances of life for our good. As His people, we are to be contented, even when our days are clouded with gloominess and unexpected career change.

When we rely on God during these tumultuous times, we can say with Paul, "I have learned to be content whatever the circumstances. I know what it is to be in need, and I know what it is to have plenty. I have learned the secret of being content in any and every situation, whether well fed or hungry, whether living in plenty or in want. I can do everything through him who gives me strength" (Philippians 4:11–13).

Sometimes, when it comes to a job transition, what we are called to do, in His strength and wisdom, is make a new plan and develop a strategy for a job search. John McDorman's career transition workshop gives us a great model for that decision-making.

In this model, we see there are four choices:

• **New Business:** Do the same kind of job, but for ourselves or a different industry.	• **New Dream:** Do a different kind of thing altogether, and strike out totally on our own.
• **New Job:** Do the same kind of job for a similar company.	• **New Career:** Do a different kind of job, but still work for a company.

If the idea of launching into the entrepreneurial category scares you to death, you're not alone. Sixty percent of job seekers choose the lower left hand quadrant: They continue doing their career, just with another company. Only a brave and well-resourced 15 percent take the leap of faith into being an entrepreneur. Regardless of what box you land in, this is still an important step in focusing your career search.

Another exercise John suggests, when we are at a point that we can truly evaluate our career focus, is to decide if we should go with "Plan A" or "Plan B." Here is how they differ:

Plan A
- A true career track
- Fulfillment through attaining our calling
- A strategy of striving for the very best we can do and be
- Our ideal job
- Making a life
- What God intended us to do all along

Plan B
- Simply our *job* track
- Paying the bills and ensuring we have benefits
- A strategy of surviving until the next better thing comes along
- Not an ideal but a *real* job
- Making a living
- The allure of the available

At some times in our lives, we all settle for Plan B. It's not the ideal, it's far from our dream, but it will do for now. Perhaps it is the part-time job well below our skills but essential to ensuring we're home when the kids get home from school. Maybe it's the assembly job in a production line, but the benefits are good and that's more important than anything else to us right now.

We have to ask ourselves, though, are we settling for second best? The God who works miracles through us may have a surprise in store when it comes to our next job move. Am I being distracted by the allure of the available when there is a "Plan A" job right around the corner, or at the very least, a "Plan B" job with a clear path to "Plan A"?

These are important issues to consider. Think through these ideas and ask yourself some tough questions before going to the Lord in prayer about your next career move. And remember that promise: He will guide us in perfect peace when our hearts are set on Him (Isaiah 26:3). That makes any job transition seem less daunting, doesn't it?

IF YOU'RE "FRESHOUT" OF SCHOOL

I would lie in bed at night, and my heart would pound like it was going to pop out of my chest. I just knew I was dying at the ripe old age of 21. A discussion of my symptoms with the family doctor revealed the true nature of my ailment: stress. I preferred to think of it as being highly alert, but no, I was totally stressed out. College graduation was a week away, and I had absolutely no idea what I would do for the rest of my life.

I had some skills and talents. I'd held a good part-time job throughout college and had a successful internship with the community affairs office of my university. I had a decent-looking résumé (for a kid), a portfolio of articles I'd written, and a few brochures I'd designed. But wow, it was really scary.

Things are a little different for today's college or technical school graduates. The placement processes are even better, and the internships and practicums often lead to real job offers, depending on the field of study. It's still a scary time to be out there job-hunting as the days of relying on mom and dad come to an end.

MEET LINDA LIVINGSTONE

Linda Livingstone is the dean of the Graziadio School of Business and Management at Pepperdine University in California. In addition to being a distinguished professor, she leads a school that is committed to developing values-centered business leaders. Pepperdine's focus on leadership grounded in core values of integrity, stewardship, compassion, and responsibility is a natural fit for Linda's faith. These values have also played an integral part of this business school's growth over the last 35 years. Today, it is one of the most admired and often recognized graduate business schools in the nation.

As she guides young people from all walks of life out the college doors and into the work world, Linda has some heart-felt, faith-filled, and business-savvy advice. Here are her four keys for career success:

As a dean, I regularly interact with women who are beginning careers (or for that matter changing careers, or trying to advance in an existing career). Three particular pieces of advice come to mind as I think about how women of faith can position themselves to experience successful and fulfilling careers.

First, identify mentors (both men and women) who have a personal interest in your development. These individuals can help you understand your strengths and weaknesses, provide advice on important challenges, and be a source of encouragement during the worst of times. They will also celebrate with you during the best of times.

Second, have the courage to act on your faith and values. Don't compromise what you believe in or who you are. God has gifted you uniquely so that you can use your talents and gifts for good works. Take full advantage of those talents and gifts in both your personal and professional life.

Third, don't be afraid to make some waves. I don't mean in a hostile or unproductive way, but rather in a way that reflects your values, faith, and integrity. And, just as important, in a way that adds value to your organization.

Fourth, follow your passion. You will spend a significant amount of time working during your lifetime. Spend this time doing something you love and something that brings joy to your life and to the lives of others. In this way, you will truly honor God and use the gifts He has given you.

So, if you are a "freshout," as we lovingly call you in the recruiting business, take heart. You are armed with your training and twenty-some-odd years of life under your belt. But more important, you have the gift of faith that will see you through this and every other major life transition that comes your way. Although some of the exercises and examples in this book may be more useful to you a few more years down the road, they will still provide you good food for thought as you build your reputation as a trusted employee and dedicated worker.

MEET MELLANIE TRUE HILLS

There is one final thing I want us to consider when it comes to managing and planning our careers. Let's make a big left turn in our discussion, literally to the left side of your body. Let me tell you the story of Mellanie True Hills and how a brush with death set her on a career track she would have never envisioned.

Mellanie was in the fast-paced, speed-obsessed high-tech industry. After being an executive at Dell in charge of the intranet, she joined an elite cadre of consultants at

Cisco who advised the top executives of Cisco's key customers on e-business strategy.

As a road warrior, those were heady times—nice hotels and restaurants, first-class upgrades, and racking up frequent flyer miles and hotel points—even though it meant being on the road about 95 percent of the time. Mellanie found it addicting to meet with executives whose faces regularly graced the covers of the top business magazines, and to bring them in for strategic discussions with Cisco's top executives. What an adrenaline rush to experience a customer CEO publicly acknowledging you and thanking you to your CEO!

With that as her routine, can you imagine Mellanie's shock when one day she found herself in the emergency room being treated for a heart attack? Mellanie was lucky—it wasn't a heart attack, though she may have only escaped one by a few hours. With a major coronary artery 95 percent blocked, they took her to surgery, where she almost died on the operating table. She survived, though, and was given a second chance.

In Mellanie's own words, "Getting a second chance changes everything. That high-profile job no longer mattered—I simply needed to stick around for my family."

The doctors couldn't explain why she had heart disease, because she didn't have the usual risk factors. She was simply overweight and overstressed—like many women—and stress wasn't even considered a risk factor for heart disease back then. Her surgeon insisted that she lose weight and eliminate her stress, or she would likely be back in three to six months for open-heart surgery.

She had to make changes quickly. As Mellanie created a plan to save her life, she found out that most women don't know that heart disease is actually the number one killer of women, stroke is the third, and that together they kill ten times as many women as breast cancer, what we perceive to be our worst enemy. We actually lose more women than men to heart problems because women have different symptoms, subtle and easily mistaken. We lose one woman every minute to heart disease and stroke in the U.S.

GOD TRULY DOES MOVE IN THE WORLD THROUGH THE HEART THAT IS FOCUSED ON HIM.

Mellanie paid attention! She felt compelled to spread the word about what she had learned about women and heart disease, so just three weeks after surgery, Mellanie made her first speech about heart disease, sharing her story with an audience of 100 women. That day set her on a new mission to raise awareness and encourage prevention of heart disease. Though she didn't know how at the time, she knew that she would be guided down a new career path.

Mellanie now speaks to corporations, organizations, and associations. She coaches individuals to create healthy lifestyles and organizations to create healthy, productive workplaces. Because she knew that most of us need a process to make it easy to create a healthier life, she spent 18 months researching and writing *A Woman's Guide to Saving Her Own Life* to provide women with the tools and processes to create a plan that can save their lives from heart disease. She sees herself now as an instrument of the Lord, with a message of hope, encouragement, and inspiration that literally saves lives.

We learn two important things from Mellanie's amazing story. One, our careers may make dramatic turns based on health issues that force striking changes in our lifestyle. Second, our health has to come first. It does not do us any good to build a golden career on a body that is teetering on the brink of failure.

Wherever you are on the nine-to-five spectrum:
   looking for the first time,
      looking for the umpteenth time,
         looking for a change, or
            looking for growth,
you've now gotten a good overview of what it means to start on the path toward growth or a job change. Your job can be a rewarding and satisfying experience, regardless of what it is. When you're on God's ordained path, no matter the occasional detour and road block and construction zone, our Father will use you to further His kingdom if you are open to be used by Him. He truly does move in the world through the heart that is focused on Him. It's your career—your choice—but your heavenly Father will use you to His glory when you make a plan, make yourself available, and remember that you are a daughter of the King.

MEET DEB DEWITT

Deb DeWitt is a technology manager with Continental Airlines in Houston. A while back, Deb had a remarkable dream. The whole story is on her Web site so I won't describe it all here; you need to read it for yourself. Check out this excerpt though:

I dreamed I was talking to a man regarding the background design of a banner I was putting together. I asked the man if he had an image of the downtown Houston skyline. He put the image of one on his monitor before me. Immediately, in my dream he and I began to travel into the image on a type of hovercraft. We first circled the downtown area perimeter. I recognized all of the buildings as we were flying by them....I noticed that as we traveled over each building, a white, fluorescent cross would top each one. Crosses began appearing on the tops of each office building.

There was such a peace and an expectancy that rose up in me—I was taken aback at the appearance of these crosses and just the glory of their beauty. The dream ended and I awoke without understanding what it was the Lord was saying to me. However, since having the dream, I understand this is the vision He has for each and every one of us as we step out into workplace ministry. One by one, you will be empowered to step out into your workplaces and proclaim His kingdom and it will be established on earth as it is in heaven.

Deb had that dream a decade ago. Today, Workplace Warriors has more than 450 members worldwide, and it is responsible for workplace ministries at companies like Continental Airlines, Shell Oil, Exxon/Mobil, Occidental Petroleum, Hess, Eggleston-Briscoe, and many others. The Workplace Warriors Web site features daily devotionals and a prayer request board, and through the site you can request help on starting workplace ministries in your corner of the world.

Do you still think ordinary women can't do extraordinary things? Deb will be the first to tell you she had a remarkable dream, but never dreamed what the Lord would do through her. That's what God is all about. By His power working in us, we are capable of, and furthermore, called, to do extraordinary things. In Ephesians 1:18–22 (italics mine), Paul prayed a remarkable prayer for the church. It still holds true for us today:

> "I pray also that the eyes of your heart may be enlightened in order that you may know the hope to which he has called you, the riches of his glorious inheritance in the saints, and his *incomparably* great power for us who believe. That power is like the working of his mighty strength, which he exerted in Christ when he raised him from the dead and seated him at his right hand in the heavenly realms, far above all rule and authority, power and dominion, and every title that can be given, not only in the present age but also in the one to come."

Did you catch that, friend? The same incomparably great power that raised Jesus from the dead is available to us. It is power that we can rely on to own and pursue careers in which we can make a difference. It is power we can rely on to make an impact in the marketplace. It is power that never runs down even when our physical batteries need recharging. Finally, it is power we can tap into regardless of our job description, position title, or career path.

LESSONS AT WORK

Think:
- What makes you tick?
- What gets you jazzed?

- What do you do that causes you at the end of the day to truly feel satisfied?
- Are you able to use those skills and abilities at work, at home, or in your volunteer efforts?
- What project or role can you pursue that will allow you to do something new? Is there a task you can tackle for the first time to spur new skill growth?
- Can you explore moving into the same type of job, but with a very different manager or team, or perhaps a new branch or location?
- How can you plan for and move in the directions of positions where your God-given talents will be used and stretched?
- Who can help you do this?

Do:
- Get some insight regarding how you function and how you operate. Study your personality, for instance. Read the book *Personality Plus* by Florence Littauer, and investigate the workplace resources that complement it at www.classservices.com.
- Write down roles either within or outside your organization, business, or industry that use your strengths and would challenge you to broaden your skills.
- Meet with people this month who do those jobs, and begin to truly understand those roles and what they require.
- After your meeting, write down what it would take to get you there and what skills you would need to polish.
- Also write down how it can benefit your employer to move you in that direction. How can this idea improve your company's competitive position, for example?

- Get feedback about your strengths from individuals you work with outside the scope of your job: your pastor or other church members, for instance. These people can often provide fresh insight into roles where your gifts can function best and your heart can be fulfilled.
- Meet with a recruiter or professional head hunter or career consultant. The price of a cup of coffee, lunch, or even a $150 investment for an hour of good career advice may be well worth it to give you a clear picture for future planning.
- Discuss with your manager the feasibility of a role change in the future, what you've explored, and why it will benefit the business.
- If your current situation appears to have little future growth, consider the possibilities of a move outside your current company or organization. When? Where? How? Is there a plan you can put in place to begin a move in that direction?
- If a move isn't feasible, geographically, financially, or otherwise, how can you begin to view what you do from eight to five as Kingdom work, not just work?

CHAPTER TWO

The Political Machine

LESSON #2
ORGANIZATIONAL POLITICS EXIST IN
EVERY COMPANY.

"Man is by nature a political animal."
—Aristotle

The political animal. The mover and shaker. The schmoozer. Hobnobbing her way through cocktail parties or committee meetings, working the crowd. The negative connotations surrounding someone considered to be political are prolific. We don't want to be known as political. But good old Webster's, the really big edition, gives us some definitions of *political* and *politics* that might make us stop and think. It uses words and phrases like *shrewd. Skillful. Ingenious in statecraft. Prudent in management. Expedient and judicious. Artful in address or procedure.* Those all sound like very useful skills regardless of our job or position. After all, I sometimes have to be *prudent in management* just to keep peace between my son and daughter, and it occasionally takes some *artful addressing* to get what I want from a customer service person!

Growing up, I thought politics was reserved for governmental elections and public leaders, and occasionally it surfaced in my mother's garden club doings. Mom hadn't worked outside the home since before I was born, but over the course of many years she was president and chairwoman of just about everything dirt- and garden-related in my hometown. I remember her on the phone late in the evenings, *ingenious in her statecraft*, negotiating some budget proposal and carefully weaving her way around municipal entities to make sure the roses and shrubs and seedlings of our city's parks were well protected from encroaching development. Mom was a deft political animal, and the botanical and horticultural citizens of Fort Worth, Texas, were better for it.

Of course any of us who attended college and found ourselves in academic organizations or service and social clubs saw politics there. In the quest to beef up future résumés and ensure there was plenty to put on upcoming job applications, the *prudent managers* took on campus leadership positions and sometimes tough topics. I marveled at those who had time to throw themselves headfirst into student government while I struggled to survive the lowest level of freshman math class.

It wasn't too much longer after college and the first few regular paychecks that I discovered that politics and political animals thrive in the workplace.

In all workplaces.

Even yours.

Even when it says in the corporate culture handbook that it isn't a political culture.

Even if it is a nonprofit organization committed to some noble cause.

Even if you work for a church or ministry among committed believers, there are politics, heaven forbid.

Because man is a political beast, and most of us have a fairly decent sized selfish streak we must constantly battle, workplaces are fraught with political maneuvering. Someone is looking out for her own gain at the expense of others. Sadly, we can't trust everyone to be concerned about the good of the whole. Some will say what others want to hear regardless of how truthful it is. Some will attempt to orchestrate circumstances in order to gain the upper hand, even when they don't deserve it.

You may wish that you could find a workplace without politics, but it doesn't exist. You may wish you could do your work while ignoring the office politics, but this is never a wise attitude. If you accept politics as the norm and learn to handle them while keeping your integrity, you will be light-years ahead in the workplace.

POLITICS IN THE BIBLE

Think the Bible doesn't have much to teach us about politics? Think again. Several interesting examples of maneuvering occur in the Bible.

Rebekah and Jacob

In Genesis 27, we read that Rebekah and her son Jacob schemed together to get the father's blessing that really belonged to Esau. Isaac in his old age and frailty fell for the deception, and the coveted blessing was given to the wrong son. This was way outside the Policy and Procedure Handbook for Ancient Jewish Families. But Isaac continued to trust God. Even after he realized what had happened, Isaac followed through on his blessing of Jacob. In Genesis 28 he spoke words of encouragement over him that any of us would crave to hear from our fathers. In spite of the mistakes, maneuvering, and deceit, God saw Isaac and Jacob in a favorable enough light to commend them in the famous hall of faith in Hebrews 11.

Rahab, the Harlot

There's another fascinating Old Testament tale about Rahab in Joshua 2. This prostitute hid the Jewish spies who were helping plan the destruction of her own city and foiled the attempts of the security guards to catch them. That was some serious political shrewdness from someone in an unlikely position! Her "career" obviously didn't get in the way of God doing His work.

Days later the walls of Jericho fell at the hollering of the faithful Israelites, and Rahab and her household were saved. Even more remarkable, Rahab shows up in the Hebrews 11 walk of faith and in Jesus' lineage in Matthew 1. Tell me that God can't use just about *any-body* with a willing heart and the ears to hear His wisdom in the midst of a complicated political situation!

Joseph and His Brothers

Remember the mean brothers of our color-coated friend Joseph? They, being insanely jealous of the favor Joseph found with their father, deftly plotted against their little brother. Their plan landed him in a desert pit, but he eventually landed a prime position on Pharaoh's staff. And who comes begging for food when a nasty famine renders them ravenous? That band of cunning brothers. When his identity is revealed and his family fed, Joseph utters some of the most significant words in Scripture for those of us who deal with workplace politics: "You intended to harm me, but God intended it for good to accomplish what is now being done..." (Genesis 50:20).

James and John's Mother

Then there's the mother of Zebedee's sons. In Matthew 20 she asks Jesus if her sons can sit on Jesus' left and right in His coming kingdom. "Can't my boys have a prime spot on Your staff?" She was clueless. "You don't know what you are asking," Jesus replies. Most of us are clueless and don't know what we're really doing when we fall into a pattern of political scheming.

We could go on and on. The Bible knows that we will all suffer the consequences of the political machine at one time or another and even find ourselves behind the wheel of it when we're not paying attention to where we're driving, but remarkably, God will use difficult situations and even ill-meaning co-workers to accomplish good things in the long run. *Truth will prevail.*

In my role as an employee relations representative, I often listened to distraught folks with tales of relationships gone sour or performance reviews that just didn't seem right. Sometimes there was a justified issue that needed attention, but more often than not, the biggest victims were the wounded egos and slighted feelings. A perspective shift was the primary perspective to help folks get back on track and focused on their jobs.

You see, when politics strike, when the wily have their way and the faithful are called to step into a tricky situation, God is at work. Countless times in my career I have seen events play out that caused untold pain and unnecessary hassle, but in the end, truth almost always prevailed and those in the right came out on top. In fact, that became my mantra in difficult employee relations situations, "Truth will prevail."

There's a downside, but there is also an upside to all things political. Go back to those words from Webster's. For instance, *shrewd*. In Matthew 10:16, Jesus reminds His disciples that He is sending them out like sheep among wolves. Sound like your last budget meeting? He tells them to be "as shrewd as snakes and as innocent as doves." The Greek word for shrewd is *fronimos*, which means intelligent or wise. So being politically astute at work isn't necessarily bad. It can mean being smart and relying on our God-inspired wisdom to handle down-right nasty situations in a manner that brings Him glory.

TO BE OR NOT TO BE—INVOLVED

Here is some encouragement from that wise guy, Solomon. Proverbs 16:7: "When a man's ways are pleasing to the LORD, he makes even his enemies live at peace with him." We are only responsible for what we do and how we respond—we simply cannot fall into the trap of always jumping into our co-workers' messes believing we can self-righteously repair the wrongs wrought during every bit of political wrangling.

As a mother, I have seen this firsthand lately. Third-grade girl politics. It's the prime training ground for many of us. My daughter plopped in the car one day and started talking, barely taking a breath between sentences. She was describing one of those, "she said then she said then her feelings got hurt and she won't be her friend unless she..." encounters. Sound vaguely familiar? My daughter had been trying to fix the problem.

I sat there with my jaw on the steering wheel wondering why this was already starting with sweet innocent nine-year-olds in a *Christian* school. I suddenly had a glimpse into the future. There was my daughter, all grown up, a middle-aged mom, and she had become—a busybody! Aaack! She thought it was her role to right the wrongs of the world, and get into everyone else's business, and tragically, she had no friends. When she stopped for a breath and a bite of a peanut butter cracker, I put my hands on her shoulders, looked intently into her giant blue eyes, and said, "I hereby proclaim you as the little girl who does not need to fix everything!" She giggled and we went on to have a conversation about politics and friendship and kindness tempered with wisdom.

My daughter had learned the Fisher-Price version of a life-altering lesson. Political situations are inevitable, and knowing that is the first step to becoming politically astute—really just another term for having wisdom. If we are wise, we will develop the spiritual ears to hear whether God is leading us out of a situation or, occasionally, to get involved.

POLITICAL SITUATIONS ARE INEVITABLE, AND KNOWING THAT IS THE FIRST STEP TO BECOMING POLITICALLY ASTUTE.

Being politically savvy is reading the nonverbal cues, listening for extreme statements, and learning to turn off our tendency to either wholeheartedly agree or disagree with any and everything we hear.

Being able to navigate around political circumstances means being able to see interconnected relationships and hidden motivations, determine your individual relationship to them, then prayerfully plan a direction or response that will allow you to be as successful as possible given the circumstances.

Sometimes, politics will mean jumping in feet-first, armed with all the power of the Holy Spirit, but most times it means getting out of the way. Don't go to the political party if you aren't invited, and if you go, remember to separate the people from the problem if at all possible.

For example, let's say that your manager keeps shifting your team's priorities in order to please her manager who keeps shifting priorities. Manager number one is up for either a promotion or a prestigious position in Europe, but she knows this is contingent on how the quarter goes. And this quarter is quickly going according to the whim of manager number two. Getting anything finished is like trying to get Jell-O to stick to a wall.

In a situation like this, it's easy to get so focused on the work you *can't* get accomplished that you fail to see what's causing the logjam. Before you hit someone in the head with the nearest log, it helps to take a step back and look at the beavers building the jam-up. Just the realization that your woes are the result of political maneuvering—not your team's lack of performance or skill—can be a stress-relieving experience. Again, it helps to remember that you can only control what you can control.

Sometimes the next step, if it's possible, is to go to your boss and frankly discuss the situation. If she is caught in a mess, she will appreciate the candor from her team members. Then together you can determine a reasonable approach to solving the problem or completing the project.

Sometimes, however, that approach itself is politically incorrect. The last thing you really want to do is talk to Ms. Shifting Priorities and then find yourself ducking into the ladies' room every time she walks down the hall.

In that case, it is what it is. In my experience, sometimes the old phrase, "leave well enough alone" applies quite nicely. Whether it was the giant company I worked for or one of the smaller organizations where I spent part of my career, I would recognize that certain things were out of my control—the egos and ambitions of those above me, for instance. I would try to focus on doing my work to the best of my ability, even if it were changed tomorrow. Those are times when it is best to take a "chill pill" and accept what we cannot manage.

As a woman saddled with the curse of competency, recognizing that I cannot control everything within my realm is not pleasant, but it is a bit of personal growth I must face daily. I can label and organize and file and administrate better than just about anybody, but there are still times when I need to just let go. Can anyone out there relate?! Can I get an, "Amen, sister"?

Dee Ann Turner, our friend from Chick-Fil-A, echoes this sentiment. "If I was ever slighted or offended at work, I'd assume it was unintentional and get on with my job. When we get focused on nursing every little issue that arises, two things happen. One, we get away from what we're being paid to do to make us and our business successful. Second, we are not allowing God to direct our path. We're not really trusting in him to keep our best interests at heart."

MEET EMMA EVANS

Here's another woman's perspective on politics. Emma Evans has served in management and leadership roles in healthcare business administration for 25 years across several states. She has experience on the payer side, with two nationally recognized insurance companies, and for the last ten years she has supported the provider side of the business, working with hospitals and physicians. Take a look at how office politics has impacted her—and her faith:

In my mid-thirties I experienced my first serious political injustice at work. My senior vice president was, in my opinion, treating a field manager very poorly. After some time, I chose a quiet Friday afternoon to take my grievance about the situation to human resources. By the end of the day the following Monday, I found myself unemployed after twelve and a half years with the company I loved. It did not occur to me to put the situation and all the people involved in God's hands through prayer. After all, I thought I could handle it! I could do my job, stand for injustice and do my vice president's job too, for that matter! Sure, I may have deserved some kind of disciplinary action, but losing my job after over a decade of devoted service and an impeccable record was severe. In my vice president's secular view though, I had committed the unforgivable sin: disloyalty. He was in the position to paint the picture the way he wanted, give or take the truth, and he did.

Nearly a decade later as the seventh victim in a serial sexual harasser's pathway I had finally learned my lesson. On my knees I prayed and literally stood on the Word of God to make the situation right, not just for me, but also for everyone involved, including the harasser's wife. Psalm 37:1–10 was my saving grace. Looking back, it is amazing to me how quickly justice came to that situation when I didn't feel like I had to step in and fix it.

Politics are in the workplace to stay and no matter how unjust, unfair, unrighteous, selfish, blindly ambitious, or evil the circumstances may be, as a Christian, like it or not, the solution begins with you. Pray earnestly over the situation and don't waste time agonizing over it. Do your work and pray, pray, pray!

I'm not suggesting that we should never respond through proper channels when wrong is being done in a workplace situation. But our first response should always be to pray, pray, pray! Then we will allow God to guide us in our choices. He may guide us to speak up or to wait. Either way, it's infinitely better to be guided by God than by our fear, anger, or ambition.

Sometimes life is not fair—not a popular opinion in a society where we are consumed with not offending anyone. But the U.S. Constitution truly does not protect us from being offended. Although life isn't fair, once more: truth will ultimately prevail. If your boss is truly a creep, then he will eventually be found out. His sales revenue or productivity in the plant won't matter anymore and he'll be gone. Then, how you've handled your conflicts with him will be even more important because his replacement will be looking for the right people to participate on a transition team.

> **IT IS INFINITELY BETTER TO BE GUIDED BY GOD THAN BY OUR FEAR, ANGER, OR AMBITION.**

Office politics offers us another unique opportunity: the chance to demonstrate otherworldly behavior in a very worldly situation. I wish I could report that I chose this path often, but in truth it only happened a few times: After dealing with a particularly nasty situation at the office, I would be approached by a co-worker asking how I did it. How did I handle such a tough conflict with grace and diplomacy and what appeared to be ease?

My response was about keeping calm in the midst of a storm through prayer and faith just like a duck sitting serenely on the lake but paddling like mad underneath. My response to the situation and to my co-worker became an opportunity to share a bit about the relevance of faith at work. When the going gets tough, the woman whose response is tempered with faith will often have good news to share.

Once again, shrewdness is needed. We must constantly rely on God for wisdom when our earthly brains have reached their limit. We must lean on Him when things get dicey and later when we are called on to give an answer for the hope that we have (1 Peter 3:15).

The promise of Romans 8:28 is a great one when it comes to tough situations at work. I don't believe Paul was thinking about office politics when he wrote that "in all things God works for the good of those who love him, who have been called according to his purpose." But then again, Paul was no stranger to the impact of politics, having written many of his letters from a jail cell under Roman guard.

Fortunately, we'll probably never find ourselves in a prison cell as a result of political wrangling at work (although sitting through operations reviews may feel like incarceration). We will, however, inevitably find ourselves in political situations, and when we are committed to glorifying God and relying on His power and wisdom, those complicated circumstances can result in significant personal, professional, and spiritual growth, not a sidetracked faith.

LESSONS AT WORK

Think:

• Who in your business tends to make the hair stand up on the back of your neck?

- What situations, circumstances, or relationships cause you to get into defense mode, ready to rumble at the least sign of a conflict or complicated circumstance?
- On the other hand, who is your ally? Is there another woman on your team or on your shift who is often the voice of reason when it comes to office politics?
- Are there cyclical times in your business when office politics get the upper hand and difficult issues seem to come out of the woodwork? Budget time? Annual goal setting?
- Think back on those circumstances and situations and consider your reactions. Are they predictable? Do you usually get sucked into the muck and mire of political fallout, or do you manage to stay above the fray? What seems to make the difference in your response?

Do:
- As far as those testy relationships are concerned, put those folks on your prayer list. Find a great, Scripture-based prayer (other than, *"Lord, smite my enemies!"*) and commit to praying for those co-workers who give you heartburn.
- Pray not just for them, but for your attitude toward them that you would be salt and light when you'd really rather throw salt and hoist your light saber.
- Prepare your heart and mind in advance when you know you're entering the twilight zone of politics. When the headquarters honchos are due for a visit or the budget analysis is looming, it's a good idea to spend more time than usual in prayer before punching the clock at the beginning of the day.

• Write down the strategies you've used in the past to keep your mouth, heart, and behavior on the straight and narrow when everything around you is collapsing into chaos. You may not think you have "strategies," but you do! When you have managed to shrewdly navigate a difficult situation, there were behaviors and actions that set that time apart from the rest. Ask God to remind you of those and give you His wisdom to make them part of your daily modus operandi.

• Partner with your ally. Share with her your desire to manage the inevitable conflicts and political tensions at work with the highest level of integrity and ask her to help you. If you frequently sit in meetings together, come up with a hand signal to remind each other to stay above board or even instant message each other with encouragement!

• If your organization or team has a mission statement or annual objectives, review them. Sometimes a refresher on what your business is all about is a great way to keep perspective when things begin to go awry. Few can argue with the corporate mandates when a meeting starts to go south due to out-of-control egos or political maneuvering.

• Fundamental to all these to-dos is prayer. Over and over again we are promised wisdom and insight if we will just ask for it. God's wisdom to deal with whatever work dishes out is ours for the asking, and it's free!

CHAPTER THREE

The Customer as Employer

LESSON #3
THERE'S ALWAYS A CUSTOMER.

"Be everywhere, do everything and
never fail to astonish the customer."
—Macy's Motto

I've earned the reputation among friends and family as "the fruit basket lady." More than once, I have given constructive and polite feedback to a hotel or restaurant manager about the customer service I've experienced—or lack thereof. I point out that I am a businesswoman who has trained individuals and teams in customer service skills and worked for companies that built reputations on service delivery. I always couch my comments in a positive light. "I thought you would want to know . . . there is a developmental opportunity for the young man at the front desk."

In almost every circumstance, I am thanked profusely. I have received everything from fruit baskets to free dinners to free nights at resorts. It's kind of fun, actually, and one of these days I figure I'll land a contract to do customer service training at some posh hotel chain!

Sam Walton, founder of Wal-Mart, said, "There is only one boss: the customer, and he can fire everybody in the company from the chairman on down, simply by spending his money somewhere else." We all need this reminder now and then, regardless of whom our customer is and what position we hold.

Aside from the profit-driven and practical business relevance of providing good service, we don't have to go very far in the Bible to read God's instruction to have a servant's heart, and to see His men and women lead through servanthood. It does not take a giant intellectual leap to apply those examples to serving customers.

In this chapter, I would like to redefine the word "customer" and encourage you to commit yourself to astonishing your customers with outstanding customer service. Sam's quote is remarkably true. Consumers have a myriad of choices as to where and how they spend their money. One bad experience at a florist, hotel chain, car rental company, or gas station can prevent a customer from ever doing business there again. And with the homogenous nature of our world—where every suburb across the country has the same neon signs and shopping malls—the savvy businessperson cannot afford to lose a customer in Dallas who then will not do business with him when traveling in Detroit, Duluth, or Deerfield.

THE CUSTOMER IS OUR BOSS

Sometimes, buried within our organizations or stuck behind a cash register or service counter, we forget that ultimately the customer is our boss. It's easy to get distracted by our own lives and business issues. But if our customer doesn't return to do business with us again and again, if she doesn't pay the bill, we don't pay our bills. A wise employee knows who her customers are, and approaches her relationships with them to develop loyalty, repeat business, and continued profit for our business. How does customer service relate to keeping our faith on track and having an impact in the marketplace?

First of all, we all have customers, regardless of our job or position. You do not have to be in sales or customer service to be in a give-and-take relationship at work. Wherever you sit on the company food chain, someone is likely relying on what you do and how well you deliver it. Your customers may be internal ones, such as members of another department or team. They may be the people inside your business for whom you develop programs or to whom you deliver mail.

An executive or a senior leader can even broaden her view to think of her entire organization as a "customer." Employees rely on her and her leadership team to make wise decisions to run the company in a way that ensures effective delivery of the product or service to the paying customer at the end of the value-profit chain.

That value-profit chain is that interconnected relationship between supplier, manufacturer, seller, distributor, and customer—and all those parts in between. The well-connected value-profit chain promotes profitability for the business and ensures satisfaction for the one paying the bills at the final link.

If you are doing the best you can to serve your "customer" wherever you fit in that value-profit chain, then the ultimate customer with a purchase order or credit card at the ready will be satisfied and will come back over and over again. If you are not focused on pleasing your customer, you become the weakest link—and ultimately may get voted off the team!

It's critical to remember that the customer who has a bad experience becomes a bane to the businessperson's existence. The old adage is true: If mama ain't happy, ain't nobody happy. And mama's going to make sure everyone *knows* she is unhappy, whether it is the auto dealer, air conditioner service person, or grocery store. How many times have you told someone when you had a great experience at a gift shop or a hotel or buying a car? Compare that to the times you have ranted and raved to anyone who would listen about the jerk who allegedly fixed your car and how you'll *never* under any circumstances return to that place of business. See what I mean?

Every year we marvel about the cost of ads during the Super Bowl—and the amount of attention they get may convince us that you have to have money to market a product well. True, advertising costs a lot of money, but the word-of-mouth advertising that comes from happy customers is priceless. It's estimated that in the banking industry, for instance, it costs five to ten times more to acquire a new customer than to keep an existing one. You do the numbers—in any business, it is more cost effective to keep them happy and coming back.

MINIMUM-WAGE CUSTOMER SERVICE

I learned about serving the customer early in my career. My first job, at a card and gift shop, was perfect for a 20-year-old. Cute cards, Christmas ornaments, and candles. I didn't make a dime. The owner of the Hallmark Haven allowed her sales staff to keep a tally of their purchases in an index card file under the counter so we could pay for them on payday. We stocked up on enough goodies to ensure that our bank accounts saw very little of our minimum-wage paychecks.

It would have been easy to slump behind the counter and wait for people to wander up to the cash register, but I soon discovered that a tidy store and a smile for everyone who walked in the door resulted in higher sales. Higher sales meant the owner was happy and I got those mind-boggling twenty-five-cent-an-hour raises to fuel my passion for sappy cards and Christmas ornaments.

The owners had two stores—and they couldn't have been in more different parts of town. Store number one was in a lower middle class suburb with almost a rural feel, and it was frequented by grandmothers who had just lunched at the cafeteria around the corner and working men rushing in at the last minute to get a card for a wife, mother, or girlfriend. I learned to provide needed assistance to the lady who couldn't see well enough to pick out a card, or give directions to Mr. Jones who came in at least twice a month but could never remember where the sympathy cards were.

Store number two was much more elegant. It was in a new, high-end shopping center in one of the preferred zip codes. These people spent money. I learned the art of suggestive selling in this posh gift shop on the west side of town. I learned how to question the customer to figure out what her true need was. What's going to make her recipient happy—and bring that customer back for another visit? A $1.25 card today often led to a $50 set of candlesticks tomorrow.

WHEN YOU TREAT THE CUSTOMER KINDLY AND WITH RESPECT, THE RESULTS GO DIRECTLY TO THE BOTTOM LINE.

Ultimately, it was about the customer. They looked vastly different, and it would have been easy to provide just the minimum: take their money and mumble a disinterested, "Thanks." But instead I learned the art and science of customer service in this tiny card shop. I discovered when you took the time to treat the customer kindly and with respect and understand what they wanted—even when they didn't really know themselves—the result went directly to the bottom line.

Many of the retail giants and boutique shops that survived our recent economic upheaval are the ones known for customer service. Here's a great example: While shopping in Nordstrom one holiday season, my youngest child was the victim of a snowstorm. While admiring a lavishly decorated Christmas tree, she decided to see what it would look like for all that shredded, glittery plastic snow to fly. A puff of air from her powerful lungs sent plastic snow crystals flying all right—right into her big blue eyes. It was not long before the tears were falling and the Nordstrom associates were flocking our way.

No fewer than three sales associates and two on-call managers were quickly hovering to ensure that this little customer was okay. A janitor came by to offer the eye wash station in back. Another manager came running with damp paper towels. I think they were just short of calling 911 when the winning offer came: that wet paper towel and a cookie from the cafe.

As we resumed our shopping, we discussed that it was a good thing the flying snow happened in Nordstrom and not some other department store *not* known for attentive personal service and customer focus. The screen saver on the point of purchase terminals at Nordstrom that day was, "Treat each customer like you would treat your best friend." That was certainly our experience.

My early lessons in retail customer service have paid off again and again throughout my career:

- Training young sales people, many in their first professional jobs
- Building rapport among community groups seeking to stem the tide of drug and alcohol abuse among kids
- Serving association members and selling ads and convention space

- Leading corporate functions with primarily *internal* customers
- Creating and maintaining relationships with clients as an entrepreneurial businesswoman

With certainty and experience I can tell you that the rule "put the customer first" impacts the profitability and ultimate success of any business. In the end, it is not only the customer, but also my business profitability and success that are at stake.

LEGENDS OF CUSTOMER SERVICE

I once worked with an individual who treated customers like interruptions. Her tone was generally curt instead of courteous, and she could have made phone-slamming an Olympic sport. She didn't get the fact that in our corporate staff positions, we still had customers. They were the employees of the company, not people buying a box or a widget, but they were still our customers. In our situation, there was no competition. They couldn't go anywhere else if they weren't happy with our services. In this case, it was not a question of losing the customer to a competitor, but it was definitely about ensuring that they would be willing to fund our services year after year.

In the early days of Dell, the stories of rescued customers were the stuff of urban legend. A technical support representative pulls the hard drive out of his own computer, drives 250 miles to a customer at 2:00 in the morning, and repairs his system before the customer's critical deadline. The remote technicians work until the wee hours to restore computer service in the rural hospital racked by a storm. A phone customer is surprised to hear, "Thanks for calling Dell, this is Michael, how can I help you?" And it wasn't just any Michael: it was the CEO himself staying in touch with the customer.

Those are the product-related customer service wins. There are also the stories of service achievements based on how we are treated as consumers, not necessarily buying a product.

We lost our seven-year-old daughter on vacation one year. Living every parent's nightmare, we exclaimed to each other: "I thought she was with you!" "Well, I thought she was with *you!*" Within minutes, no fewer than 20 radio-equipped staffers from the family resort were scouting the vicinity for our little one. By then, she'd already followed her well-practiced plan and told "someone with a name badge" that she was lost. When we caught up with her, she was happily sipping a soda at the poolside restaurant, waiting for her weak-kneed parents to arrive. Surrounded by two pool attendants, a security manager, the concierge, and three waitresses, she was fine. We were forever grateful for the care and concern shown to our little one and her frantic parents. That hotel chain moved up several notches in my book that day.

The stories I could tell are endless, but all end one of two ways: satisfied and delighted customers willing to tell their tale, or unhappy and disgruntled consumers ready to blast out warnings on the World Wide Web. In either scenario, the characters and requirements are the same: buyers and consumers who demand excellent service from the businesses they deal with.

INTERNAL CUSTOMERS

Some of us are corporate staff members in large corporations. We work in finance, human resources, legal, or administrative functions. In any business, the corporate or administrative staff is overhead. We have to justify our existence every day (or at least every budget cycle). Our customers are the teams that do the real work of designing, marketing, building, and selling products or services. As members of these functions, we can actually consider the *whole company* our customer. What we do and how effectively and efficiently we deliver it, whether we keep our promises and commitments, affects others' ability to do their work. And that ultimately affects the customer who calls in with an order for actual product.

Smart organizations and leaders pay attention not only to the satisfaction of their paying customers—measured by sales and repeat business—they pay attention also to the satisfaction and loyalty of internal customers. I know of an internal legal team that sent out customer service surveys to "clients" within its own company. Now when *lawyers* want to know how well they're doing, that's remarkable commitment to the internal customer! When those leaders actually change behavior and refocus efforts of their staff *as a result* of that customer service survey, that's astonishing, as Macy would say.

FOR THE SELF-EMPLOYED

Building and maintaining customer relationships is no less important for the self-employed and no less challenging. We don't see our customers everyday. We don't hear from them often. But staying in touch with those who have been clients in the past and potentially will do business with us in the future is critical.

Managing client relationships is more than an occasional e-mail or holiday card. For the self-employed, it is about demonstrating how we add value and keeping our services top-of-mind with busy people. E-mail is a great way to offer tips and "free" newsletters that highlight products and beneficial offerings. Dropping a copy of a relevant article in the mail with a business card attached shows we're thinking of our client and we understand what her needs are.

The classic example is the calendar sent out by the insurance agent at the beginning of the year. It is a nice touch and a reminder to pay those premiums on time. One of my associates is a very successful human resources consultant. He uses his e-mail contact list to periodically send out articles he has authored. The kicker: each article is *to be continued…* The reader is always waiting to hear what Bill has to say next time about "the business of HR."

Asking for feedback when we finish a project—or lose one to a competitor—shows we are focused on pleasing those who pay the bills. And that is a trait that is too often lacking among the harried, self-employed businessperson or working-from-home mom. These folks barely have time to complete their work, much less think of the meaningful details that build client relationships. But a note to a customer when it is least expected is kind of like a love note in your kids' lunch box: At the time it may not mean much, but in the future they will remember your thoughtfulness and care.

For front-line sales and service people, the need to take care of our customer is obvious. On my "route," that well traveled path between school, church, grocery store, and dry cleaners, there are two large chain drug-stores, right across the street from each other, of course. But I only shop at one of them. Why? Because of Susie. Susie always has a grin on her face and something kind to say. She says, "Hi, how ya doin'?" and sounds like she means it! She'll chat about my purchases and ask, "Do ya like that brand of air freshener? I've never tried it!"

THE CUSTOMER IS ULTIMATELY YOUR EMPLOYER.

She may never make a million dollars and never sit in a corner office, but Susie has an impact. Who knows how many harried moms or worn-out businessmen leave her counter after a long day just a little happier because of her smile and friendly attitude. She's a good reminder to those of us who deal daily with customers that our actions, attitudes, and behaviors are significant.

The customer may be internal or external. You may be a retail clerk, a service provider, a cog in some corporate wheel, or a self-employed sales rep. Regardless, you have a customer to be nurtured, and that customer is ultimately your employer. When you adopt this attitude and its related behaviors, your career picks up, and so do sales and repeat business.

THE BIBLE KNOWS SERVICE

It is not just about your own career success and increased profits, though. These are attitudes and behaviors so consistently supported by Scripture that it is difficult to choose among all the possible verses to cite.

First of all, there's the classic "golden rule" taken from Jesus' words in the Gospels. Mom taught it to us when we came home from school crying about the bully on the playground, and it still holds true today: "Do to others what you would have them do to you" (Matthew 7:12).

Then there are the myriad of exhortations to put others first and serve. Service is our opportunity to reflect God's love and grace even in a workplace where we might not be able to talk freely about our relationship with Him. "Serve wholeheartedly, as if you were serving the Lord, not men, because you know that the Lord will reward everyone for whatever good he does" (Ephesians 6:7–8). "Each one should use whatever gift he has received to serve others, faithfully administering God's grace in its various forms" (1 Peter 4:10).

And finally, we have the frequent and humbling reminders that Jesus Himself came as not as a warrior king, but as a servant. He could have called down the armies of heaven every time the crowd jeered, every time a stone was thrown, but He didn't because He chose to serve so we might live. Matthew 20:28 summarizes it this way: "Just as the Son of Man did not come to be served, but to serve."

Jesus' power-in-humility is probably best summed up in Philippians 2:8–11: "And being found in appearance as a man, he humbled himself and became obedient to death—even death on a cross! Therefore God exalted him to the highest place and gave him the name that is above every name, that at the name of Jesus every knee should bow, in heaven and on earth and under the earth, and every tongue confess that Jesus Christ is Lord, to the glory of God the Father."

On one level, customer services is about profitability and repeat business and high scores on customer satisfaction surveys. On a much deeper and more important level though, it is about humility and servanthood and demonstrating grace and kindness to those who sometimes least deserve it:

- The grouchy lady who wanted turquoise, not aquamarine towels
- The tired mom who wanted the orthodontist appointment on Tuesday not Friday
- The harried father who needed his car fixed yesterday not today
- The manufacturing manager who needed the parts shipped by noon, not five

As people of faith, we have the advantage of the Holy Spirit to help us when we don't feel like being nice. Even organizations with a ministry focus need to rely on this strength sometimes.

MEET MARITA LITTAUER

Marita Littauer is the President of CLASServices (Christian Leaders, Authors, and Speakers Services). She and her phenomenal mother, Florence Littauer, are the reasons I have two book contracts. They help people launch Christian writing and speaking careers through training courses, networking, and publicity consulting. CLASS is also a speakers' bureau for organizations looking for both inspirational and business related speakers. Take a look at what Marita thinks about customer service:

> Though my business is more ministry than business, I still think we need to focus on customer service—in fact, more so. While some Christians think they can take short cuts or

save God money, I believe that we need to do things better than those in the world. In my 20-plus years in Christian ministry, I have been appalled, as I have interacted with many major Christian organizations at their total lack of customer service, let alone the love of the Lord.

To me, customer service is an overflow of our faith. When people call CLASS I want them to feel glad that they called, that Jesus has hugged them. From my experience with other organizations, I find that the service a customer receives is a reflection of the attitude at the top. I train my staff that even the way we answer the phone matters. Whether folks call CLASS to register for a conference, place an order, book a speaker—or just to get answers to their questions—they deserve the utmost respect and highest level of service. Yes, sometimes someone in our office has a bad day and despite our best efforts, we do make mistakes, but we always remember that these 'nice and forgiving' Christians who are our customers can take their business somewhere else. We truly want our customers to feel valued. Give our offices a call and put us to the test.

MEET DARLEEN REESE

In another field entirely is Darleen Reese. Darleen runs Christian Brothers Automotive in Brentwood, Tennessee. She and her husband opened this franchise in September 2000 and now Darleen is in charge. Automotive repair is not a typical business endeavor for a woman, but Darleen has been surprised at the way God has grown her, and given her opportunities to minister to the people who are her customers and employees.

"I was home raising kids for a long time," she says. "Being in the marketplace has helped me reconnect with the struggles people have." Considering the fact that an individual's interaction with the car repair shop is usually based on a crisis, Darleen sees plenty of struggling people. "Customer service is a lost art," remarks Darleen. "In the automotive service industry it is really important because when customers walk in the door they are about to be out of their car for a period of time. That in and of itself presents stress for most people."

Darleen is usually the one to drive customers from the shop where they've left their four-wheeled baby back to their workplace or home. During these drives she's able to really build relationships and show empathy and concern for her customers. "We are so focused on building relationships and creating trust. We have to be because most people don't understand what we are doing when we are under the hood of their car. Sincerely caring for people is essential so our customers know that we are interested in them as a person, not just in having their business. It is how we build that critical level of trust so they believe us when we tell them what we have to do to their car."

Indeed, making sure a customer understands what is going on is a crucial piece of the customer service puzzle. In any field where repair is necessary, ensuring our customers truly know what is broken and what must be fixed is essential.

You put gas in it and it starts. That's the extent of my knowledge about cars. If control-alt-delete doesn't make my computer work when it hangs up, I'm out of options and I call for help. When any major kitchen appliance starts to make more noise than the children, I shut off the power and grab the yellow pages. I'm not unlike most consumers and therefore deserve to have relationships with service people where there is mutual trust and respect.

Darleen has seen this play out again and again in her service business. Relationships matter. See for yourself what she's talking about. Take a look at this story.

When we first opened, we repaired a customer's car just before he left on vacation. We didn't know at the time that the repair we completed often led to another problem with that particular vehicle. The manufacturer's service alert had not been issued yet on that specific situation, so we genuinely had no way of knowing.

Well, sure enough, our customer went on vacation and was out of the state when his car broke down. Needless to say, he was very unhappy. We paid for a rental car so he could continue on his trip and paid to have a tow truck bring his car back to us. We went out of our way to make sure he understood that we had not purposely created a problem and explained what we had just learned from the auto manufacturer.

In the long run, he's become one of our best customers because we treated him right and made sure he understood the situation. He is a total advocate for our shop now. If we hadn't done the right thing, that could have been a disastrous situation, especially since we had just opened.

Darleen is blessed. She's a franchisee of a company committed to Christian values and operational excellence in an industry fraught with service problems and mistrust on the part of consumers. I am a customer of the Christian Brothers Automotive in my neighborhood too.

I can attest to their commitment to exemplary service and caring about me as an individual.

When I drop by for an oil change or to have a light bulb replaced, I'm greeted with, "Hey, Mrs. Baker! How are your kids? How's Wayne?" Before the discussion turns to the car, it is first about my family and me. Steve and Barbara Berry demonstrate their love of God through their interaction with people, as does Darleen Reese.

Barbara also has given rides home to busy moms with broken-down cars. Once she waited while a distraught mom fixed her kids lunch, and together they made sure it got to the child's school. Steve and Barbara have a philosophy of business that would make even the most frustrated car owner breathe a sigh of relief: Steve says, "Ultimately we will have to give an account of our lives to God. He will not be asking us 'How many cars did you fix?' or 'How much money did you make?' but He will ask 'How did you treat My most precious creation?'"

Just because it's a Christian business doesn't mean there aren't occasionally problems, though. Darleen brings up a critical point about service: "Sometimes customers get angry with us when we tell them what's wrong with their car. We try to defuse that anger with the facts about the nature of the problem and by showing empathy. In this day and age, no one wants to be without her car. We know how hard that is and really try to show compassion."

Darleen is a businesswoman, but first and foremost she is a wife and mother. "That's my priority and I use that to connect with people." She recounted a story about taking a young mother with four little ones back home while her shop repaired the car. "She was about to pull her hair out. Life is so physical when your kids are young. I had the opportunity to share with her and give her some encouragement because we are well past that stage. She seemed really relieved to hear that someone understood where she was in life and how hard it was." All that and her car was fixed too!

Remember our discussion at the opening of the chapter: that even the top brass has customers? Well, Darleen certainly gets this point. "Although I get to do the shuttling of our stranded customers and sometimes help at the counter, the main people who work with our customers are the front counter and parts guys and the technicians. Therefore I believe it is important for me to encourage them and to jump when there is some way I can help them." This is the two-sided coin of customer services: taking care of the internal and external customers.

As believers who are in business, our impact in the workplace can be measured in much more than sales quotas and service stars and repeat business. By committing to serve our customers as *people*, not just for the sake of our company and its profits but for the sake of the Kingdom, we can give others a chance to grasp a glimmer of God's grace in the mundane, daily-ness of life. At the end of the day, that's worth far more than any service award or earthly accolade, and it demonstrates once again that our faith need not be sidetracked by our work.

LESSONS AT WORK

The following ideas are taken from my workshop, The Loyalty Link: a new look at the customer relationship. In these lessons at work, there are things for you to think about, do, and honestly evaluate when it comes to your business and how you operate.

Think:

• Who are your customers? Even the ones you may not be "selling" to? Who do you support or to whom do you provide a service?

• If you are in a sales relationship, what do you do between sales cycles to maintain and build rapport?

• How can you demonstrate to your customers that you value the relationship—even if you are not currently involved in a sales cycle with them?

• What was the biggest mistake you ever made with one of your customers, and in hindsight, what did you learn from it?

Do:

• The next time you get a call from a survey company assessing your satisfaction with a service or product you purchased, take the time to answer the call. You might learn something about how to survey your own customers.

• If you're in management or another position where you don't frequently interact with end-user customers, go out on a sales call or sit down and listen in on the customer service phone lines. It'll help you reconnect with what your business is all about.

- If you sell a product, especially one that has to be assembled or otherwise configured by the end user, go buy one. Take it out of the box. Put it together, plug it in, and use it. Put yourself in your customer's shoes.
- If you serve internal customers (if you are a lawyer, CPA, marketer, or so forth) consider doing a quick customer satisfaction survey. Borrow the one your company uses with customers and make it fit your services. You'll be surprised at the insight you will gain—and remember, a complaint is a gift.

Evaluate:

- What are your business's top three competitive advantages? Even if you are the clerk in the local gas station, there are things you can identify that set your place of business apart: location, perhaps, or the selection of goodies and snacks. If it looks the same as the shop across the street, then how can you help differentiate your location purely on service?
- When was the last time you said to yourself, "I'll *never* go there again to do business!" Why? Have you ever demonstrated those same service mistakes that drove you away?
- Think about the telephone and how you can use calls to and from your customers to build positive rapport. If you can, put a little mirror on your telephone so you can smile at yourself when you pick up the phone. Believe it or not, customers will hear the smile in your voice.
- When using the telephone, think about speed, inflection, and tone of your voice. What's appropriate? Twang or no twang? Drawl or no drawl? Being from Texas, this

is one I appreciate; I've learned to say "you guys" when I call the east or west coast.

- Phrases to avoid in customer service interactions:
  "I don't know."
  "You can't do that."
  "We can't do that."
  "Just a second." (Nothing takes just a second!)
- Evaluate the catch phrases you hear yourself using, and decide if they really build relationships and show empathy.

I could go on and on. The point is, there may be a time when you need to invest in some formal customer service training either for yourself or your team. It is a worthwhile investment, because how we treat our customers goes a long way toward how we are able to show God's love in the marketplace. Jesus was all about building relationships and showing people He understood them wherever they were. Extraordinary customer service is the same—not to be served, but to serve.

CHAPTER FOUR

Job Title Terror

LESSON #4
YOU ARE NOT DEFINED BY THE TITLE ON YOUR BUSINESS CARD.

"Oh that lovely title, ex-president."
—Dwight D. Eisenhower

The job title: a moniker, a label, or an identity on a little rectangle of cardstock that allegedly tells worlds about who we are and what we do. It is a concept we latch onto early in life when we first begin to utter words like, "I want to be a nurse!" or "I want to be a fireman!" or the best one yet I've heard from my petite daughter, *"I want to drive a dump truck!"* More power to ya, honey, but they're hard to park.

From our earliest days we begin associating value with what we may or may not do for a living. As a mother of two trying to raise enlightened children, I wrestle with this constantly. I want them to be free to be who God created them to be—to seek and follow His calling on their lives—but please, Lord, let it be something at least a little prestigious and somewhat stable! Okay? I mean, they have to be able to support themselves!

When I think about the whole subject, my own ego moves in and the tough lessons I've learned about our true value and work go out the window. For instance, I have terrifying images of my son struggling to be a professional skateboarder or snowboarder! Or I imagine my daughter waiting tables in Nashville as she tries to break in to the recording business. As a mother and a woman writing a book for women from all walks of the workplace, how do I teach others to pursue their highest dreams yet at the same time not latch onto the world's view of success?

It's a tough balancing act. I learned the hard way that I was not defined by the title on my business card, and it is perfectly normal for one's scope of influence to shift throughout the life of a career. My prayer is that my personal lessons and the thoughts of other women who have experienced similar transitions will broaden your perspective and shift your paradigm.

WHAT'S IN A NAME?

The whole concept of the job title has gone through a significant shift in the past few decades. I remember working as a volunteer at the local hospital while I was in high school. This was in the 1970s and we were just entering the phase when "janitors" were becoming "environmental technicians" and "garbage men" were renamed "sanitary engineers." It was but a glimmer of what was to come.

As companies and governmental entities became larger and more complicated, more and more titles and levels were invented to represent all the shades of gray between one grade or level and another. An occupational site on the internet provides fascinating insight (if you're having trouble sleeping) on more than 1,500 job families and titles. Those are just job families, mind you. There are actual job titles buried within many of those job families! Ever hear of a brattice builder? Me neither. They build air ducts to transport air into workplaces. Oh, of course! Sounds quite essential, actually!

So the list of job titles grew and grew and grew, and then another phenomenon occurred. The working mother. Well, duh, all mothers are working mothers, so now we had to add "mothers who work outside the home" to our jargon. This is still pretty goofy when you consider that you can sign up for so many activities at your kids' school or at your church that you wouldn't have time to either work at home or have a paying job if you wanted one. I saw a bumper sticker the other day that read, "Somebody stop me before I volunteer again!"

Anyway, you see where we are going. As a society, we are very concerned with what we do and what we are called. This trend extends to all generations. Consider the other bevy of bumper stickers proclaiming "My child is an honor student at…" and "My kid can beat up your honor student…" and (my personal favorite) "My Labrador is smarter than your honor student." Well, woof to you too! Is it any wonder our kids are growing up stressed when the pressure to succeed starts so early?

I suppose because I worked so much while I was in college, I started my career with a slight advantage. My first "real" job out of the university was in a managerial position. Some have called me a born leader. My husband just thinks I was born bossy! Whatever, it worked to get me on a fast track. My second job had "director" in the title and it came with lots of travel and the chance to meet some pretty impressive people, including First Lady Nancy Reagan. My third career position also had "director" on the business card, so I figured I was really a hot shot at the ripe old age of 25.

When I went to work at Dell in 1989, I was the one of the company's first training managers. I was tasked with creating the rapidly growing computer maker's sales training programs. It was during a time when a new recruit in the sales force was handed a telecommunications head set, a price list, and told emphatically, "Answer the phone!" That was the extent of sales training at Dell in 1989.

My career there took many fascinating directions, all within human resources or internal communications. When I became pregnant with our first child, I took my first non-people management position and discovered the wonderful world of being an "individual contributor." This is a politically correct term for all sorts of positions without direct reports and management responsibility. Individual contributors can sit all throughout a company's food chain. However, the higher level individual contributor positions are generally reserved for genius technical types that you don't *want* managing people. You just keep them in darkened cubicles where they thrive under artificial light and the promise of patent awards.

When I returned to work after time off with the baby and vacation, I slowly went back into management mode and took on more responsibility until baby number two came around in 1991. At that point, I was managing the human resources function for the product development organization. That's where we kept a lot of those really smart people who thrived in artificial light and used words like *gigabyte* and phrases like "aspect oriented software development." *Whatever.* Half the time I felt like I was in a foreign country and did not know the language, but I had fun trying to keep up with them and acting like I knew what they were talking about.

I was on a team with about a dozen men (directors, vice presidents, and one senior vice president) and one woman. She was a very serious MBA with a fast track into product development management. We did not really relate to each other. I waited as long as I possibly could before I told all of them that I was expecting.

I decided to mess with their minds a little and made my proclamation in the form of a "product launch announcement" during a staff meeting. I used words like project managers (myself and my husband) and projected launch date. They were clueless. Finally, the generally reserved but at least female MBA shouted, "She's pregnant, you goofballs!"

YOUR SCOPE OF INFLUENCE WILL WAX AND WANE THROUGHOUT YOUR CAREER.

I finished out my term (literally) with them and headed back into an individual contributor role, this time working part time at home and part time in the office until I had my household humming smoothly and both the baby and the four-year-old were well acclimated to the precious child care provider who came to our home daily, toting her own toddler.

It was a pattern that would continue throughout the remainder of my career at Dell. Manager to individual contributor. Running a team to running a project. Back and forth, occasionally up and often sideways. In the midst of it all was the coveted promotion to director. Most felt it was long overdue and the congratulatory e-mails I got spanned the company directory. I'd been there a long time and had put my heart and soul into the company and felt I really deserved the promotion.

The job was a blast. I hired a new team and took on a long overdue project, running a function I knew nothing about but thinking I'd hired the right people to help us be successful. In many aspects we were. We saved a lot of money on a certain process and launched some online technology that was pretty neat. I got to do a little of what I did best—write—and delegate a lot! By this time, my mother was talking to her friends about me as if I was a personal advisor to Michael Dell himself and he wouldn't make a single decision without consulting me. My dad was starting to think of Michael Dell as the son he'd never had. They were way beyond proud of me.

DIDN'T SEE IT COMING

Our function was in a whirlwind of change at the time, though. If I'd seen it coming, I might have chosen a different path, but when the job title stars are glimmering in our eyes, we often don't see that clearly. Several significant leadership changes occurred and I found myself in the midst of a huge reorganization without a sponsor. Ah, the sponsor. That high level individual who's willing to go to bat for you at all costs. Handy to have. Risky to rely upon.

I felt the boat starting to rock before it capsized completely, but the shock of the water was still severe. My job was eliminated. "No problem, Amy, you're still very valuable to us and we don't want you to leave, but there's not another director level position at the moment that you are suitable for."

I was devastated. The poor guy who had to tell me, my interim director, felt awful too and let me go home for the rest of the day. I tracked my husband down. He was doing some painting and, while I sobbed, he slung paint around, angry that anyone would do anything to hurt his wife.

I fought the decision for a while. After the emotional shock wore off, I started my fact-based campaign listing my accomplishments: the money saved, the team hired, the projects completed. I cited the congratulatory emails and all the people who thought my initial promotion was such a good idea. I even considered playing the sexual discrimination card but stopped short of that route, probably thanks to the nudging of the Holy Spirit.

Truth be told, it was more than nudging. One day I woke up and thought to myself, *Why are you fighting for this? Why is it so important? It is just a job!* True enough. The company at that point had overall done the right thing. They kept my salary whole and didn't change many of my benefits. They announced my position change with a tremendous amount of diplomacy and grace and never ever used the word *demotion*. Yes, on some levels it was a mess, and it was political, and it was very hard, but it was handled as well as could be expected and I still had a great career.

So get over it already, and move on.

Over the course of the next several weeks, I slowly began to get my feet back on the ground and I threw myself into my new position with new challenges and opportunities. As I settled into a new routine, I also began to reflect on what I had learned during the whole ordeal. When I finally shut up long enough to listen, God taught me some valuable lessons.

- I am not defined by the title on my business card.
- My scope of influence will wax and wane throughout my career.
- My career path must be tied to God's timing, not just mine.

Overall, it was a situation that matured me. I hate those. They are never easy. I am reminded of Ephesians 4:12–13 where Paul has listed some of the jobs of believers: evangelists, prophets, teachers, and the like. The goal? "We all reach unity in the faith and in the knowledge of the Son of God and become *mature*, attaining to the whole measure of the fullness of Christ" (italics mine). There's that word, *maturity*. Paul is saying to us, "Grow up!"

The first major growing-up lesson I learned from my job title terror was that I had become way too attached to that executive position. It had begun to define me. As a Christian, I'd always said that my relationship with the Lord came before all else. I had always professed that I was defined by being His child—my identity came from being His creation. But "successful high-tech executive" had taken a predominant place in my thought life. Like the frog that cooks before he realizes he is in hot water, I had slipped into an unhealthy zone of prestigious titles and fancy parties, and had become callused from rubbing elbows with the corporate elite.

Psalm 139 is the definitive chapter in the Bible to remind us of whose we are and how we were created. How can anyone balk at phrases like "fearfully and wonderfully made" or "his works are wonderful"? Daughter of the King, those words written by King David about all God's children are *not* dependent on the business cards we carry in our Dooney and Burke or Wal-Mart sale handbag.

Is there anything wrong with holding an esteemed position at a high flying company? Absolutely not. Is it bad to achieve executive ranks among well respected leaders in any industry? No way. It is a fabulous blessing to behold, but it so easily slips out of perspective. We have to guard our hearts.

Jesus said it was easier for a camel to go through the eye of a needle than for a rich man to get to heaven. Maybe that's because the rich man's head gets too big to pass through the pearly gates! What the Lord is really teaching is the matter of perspective. The problem is when something becomes so important to us that it shifts our focus from the Father, who loves us beyond words. That certainly happened to me.

Do I believe God purposefully took away my fancy job title to teach me a lesson? No. Some might think He did, but I don't think God sends down corporately delivered missives from heaven to hurt our hearts and break our spirits. Do I think He used the situation to draw me closer to Him, though? Yes. Absolutely yes.

WAXING AND WANING

The lesson of the tantalizing but temporary title is tied to another thing I learned many times over the course of my career in several different industries and roles. Our sphere of influence waxes and wanes throughout our working lives, just as our influence shifts with our children as our parental roles change. I call it the morphing scope of influence.

It is an interesting study in career dynamics when you pull away from it and look at it from 30,000 feet. Here are some highlights from my own career story:

- Appearing on a nationally televised newscast at 24
- Meeting a first lady at 25
- Representing my state at an international conference in Sweden shortly thereafter
- Sharing the podium at conferences with NFL stars and up-and-coming presidential cabinet members

- Writing presentations for the CEO of one of the fastest growing companies in the world

And then...
- Stuffing brochures into envelopes because I'd lost my administrative help
- Delivering T-shirts to remote office buildings in the dead of night because no one else would do it
- Implementing unwanted programs for influential people that nobody would say no to and later watching a year's worth of work vanish into the ether

And back again...
- Developing mission-critical worldwide messaging for significant corporate events
- Being blessed with two book contract offers within three weeks

Wax and wane. Expand and contract. Such is the life of a working woman. Sometimes we are giddy with power and prestige (or the perception thereof), and other times we're laughing to ourselves thinking, *I went to college for this*?!

Early in my days at Dell both my husband and I had frequent access to the senior leadership of the company. My in-box was often filled with messages and requests from some of the top people. My husband, the second employee hired into Dell's advertising department, experienced the same thing. Long ago, the head honchos approved every bit of advertising before it hit the press, and Wayne had to get the signatures on the dotted lines every week.

As the company and our careers changed, that access and interaction with the big guns was relegated to company parties and occasional town hall meetings or "Hey, how's it goin'?" in the hall. It didn't mean we were less important or that what we had to contribute was necessarily less significant, but for the time being at least, our scope of influence had gone the way of the shrinky dink. A smaller image of what it used to be.

Both of us also experienced the expansion of that influence again as roles and careers changed.

It will never stop. It's a job-related morphing that will rise and fall as our economy changes, as industries merge and collapse and rebuild. It's a natural course of career management and one we must all learn to deal with. The reduction of our influence does not correlate to a reduction in our worth. If we have the perception that our sphere of influence must always grow, we will be disenchanted and frustrated in this age of restructurings, outsourcings, downsizings, and other-ings.

THE REDUCTION OF OUR INFLUENCE DOES NOT CORRELATE TO A REDUCTION IN OUR WORTH.

Furthermore, although our companies or businesses may think they rule over us, they really don't. Your company may feel omniscient, but it isn't! More often than not, our heavenly Father uses circumstances and situations that occur in our jobs to make sure we are where *He* wants us to be when *He* wants us to be there. My significant change in responsibilities at Dell, it turned out, was closely tied to a momentous change in my personal life: the aging and eventual death of both my parents.

TIMING IS EVERYTHING

In Proverbs 16:9 we are reminded, "In his heart a man plans his course, but the LORD determines his steps." It is one of many Scriptures that remind us of the value of planning—and the ultimate sovereignty of God. As I look back on what I went through as my career shifted back and forth during my days at Dell and elsewhere, I am amazed at the timing of it all.

I know many women who walked away from prestigious corporate careers to pursue what seemed like less glamorous jobs, only to find that even greater blessing and fulfillment came with that change in business card. Others never even pursued the glamour of the jet set career and haven't regretted it one bit.

My friend Jo Ann used to run the mail room in a big company. It was a dynamic place where people moved so often they just stashed their office supplies in a box. Keeping track of all these people in order to get them their mail and necessary office deliveries was next to impossible. On top of that, she managed a group of very young people, many with little work experience. She called herself the dorm mother. She counseled many a young woman through a broken heart and helped several ambitious young people transition to bigger and better jobs. Jo Ann made good money too. She had fabulous benefits and that influence thing going—regular contact with some mighty powerful people (probably more than she really wanted!). But after quite a few years, she knew it was time to go.

Today, Jo Ann cuts fabric at the local sewing and crafts store. She's bailed me out with creative ideas more than once when I needed a knight or knave costume at the last minute. Gone are the days of important meetings and hobnobbing at management confabs and training in the latest in mail room management technology. But Jo Ann is having a blast. She long ago learned that management at a big company was not all it was cracked up to be. She traded her embossed business card for a pair of engraved fabric shears, and now she dons a denim apron and comfortable shoes. She couldn't be happier.

Oh, and about God's timing—timing was a big deal with Jo Ann too…without the terror of that big job title she has more free time with some really cute grandkids.

MEET ADRIANE BROWN

Timing played into the role change that Adriane Brown experienced too. After a very successful career with one of those giant Three Initial Companies, she traded in that business card for the title of stay-home mom and business partner. Now she works part time, helping her husband run not one but two businesses. The corporate jet-setting from one city to another has stopped for the time being, but this family is seeing the rich rewards of following God's plan and trusting Him with their careers, business, and finances.

As you read Adriane's story, take note of her faith and contentedness.

> When we all but went under a few years ago, I thought we'd lost our minds. Here we both left great jobs with all the salary, benefits, and perks you could imagine, and now we were teetering on the edge of bankruptcy. God was so faithful though. We hit a new level of humility, pushed our faith to a deeper level, and trusted Him with our businesses. In His mighty power, He proved faithful and our

businesses are thriving. I don't miss my "important" corporate job at all anymore. I know I am where I am supposed to be, partnering with my husband to raise our kids and build our businesses.

It's the fundamental message of thriving through job title terror—managing the inevitable shifts that come in our careers whether they are instigated by our companies or us. "I know I am where I am supposed to be." Adriane put it perfectly.

When we know who we are in Christ and when we are seeking to fulfill His call on our lives, we will be where we are supposed to be. "'I know the plans I have for you,' declares the Lord," in Jeremiah 29:11. Those plans at times may include engraved desk sets, unlimited expense accounts, and first-class business travel. At other times, they may call for worn-out blue jeans and scrubbing baseboards in the newly rented warehouse you hope your new venture can afford. Your manicured nails may take a beating opening your own boxes as you start a new business enterprise, but nails grow back. Careers bounce back. Jobs come full circle, and what seemed like all-important, prestigious roles have a way of receding into the past when we see the promise of our future.

So the lessons of managing job title terror are:
• We are not defined by what is on our business card, or whether or not we even have one!
• Our scope of influence is likely to shift and change throughout our careers.
• God's timing is much more perfect than ours, even though we don't always understand it at the time.

The next time you catch yourself becoming insanely jealous of the co-worker who just got a promotion, or disillusioned because your job is shrinking, not growing, remember the words of Paul in Philippians 3:13–14: "Forgetting what is behind, and straining toward what is ahead, I press on toward the goal to win the prize for which God has called me heavenward in Christ Jesus."

I once heard a sermon on this Scripture titled, "Don't Park Here." We were encouraged to not park beside our past or park beside our successes but to keep focused on our heavenly calling. When that is our perspective, our job title takes a backseat. We are part of something bigger and resident of a heavenly home not subject to the whims and politics of earth-bound bosses. We ultimately work for a great and loving God who has our best interests at heart. I'll choose that career path over the world's definition of success any day.

LESSONS AT WORK

This chapter's lessons are more about thinking than doing for a change. I thought I'd give you a break! No homework—just some things to ponder over your next cup of coffee.

• On a scale of one to ten, where do you fall on the "worshipping job titles" continuum? It is great to set lofty goals, but have your goals gotten the upper hand and begun to define you?

• Have you ever caught yourself saying, "If only I get XYZ position, then I will be happy?" It's time to hit the attitude reset button!

• How do you react when others are promoted or receive accolades at work? Do you rejoice, steam internally or worse, snarl on the outside? Showing genuine excitement for others when they succeed is a surefire way of reflecting the character of Jesus at work.

• Can you see patterns in your own career where your scope of influence has grown, only to shrink again, then grow one more time? Begin to see these as normal occurrences in a dynamic business environment, and enjoy the times the job (and its stresses) are a little smaller.

CHAPTER FIVE

The Magic of Mentoring

LESSON #5
MENTORING CAN BE MAGICAL,
BUT NOT MANUFACTURED.

---

*"Keep away from people who try to belittle your ambitions.
Small people always do that, but the really great make you
feel that you, too, can become great."*
—Mark Twain

The first managers I had during my first job out of college, my first real career position, were almost as opposite as those two card shops I mentioned earlier. My direct manager was a fatherly, bearded fellow who had been in his industry more years than I'd been on the planet. He taught me the technicalities of my job. He was the consummate content expert who'd done the same type of job all his life.

My vice president was a feisty, platinum blonde career woman with a steely determination and directness I'd never seen in anyone before. She was the ever-networking, always-hustling professional. She was busting glass ceilings and making a name for herself in her industry long before anyone would openly discuss those glass ceilings and the unspoken good-old-boy-ness of most organizations. She was the one who took me to lunch in the executive dining room, just so I would "be seen," and gave me her personal guidance and tips for success.

In spite of their dramatic differences, they both had things to teach a wet-behind-the-ears manager and fledgling professional woman. Because of them and their dramatically different personalities and styles, I learned to look for what I can learn from anyone who crosses my path, to seek out mentors even if they can only guide me in one aspect of my career.

MENTORING IS NETWORKING

Mentoring and networking are both words thrown around today like old socks. Everyone tends to assume that we know what mentoring and networking mean, but I hope to broaden your perspective about these concepts so they truly benefit your career.

Where do we get the idea for mentoring anyway? Well, believe it or not, we have that famous writer and philosopher Homer to thank. In Homer's *Odyssey*, Odysseus holds a guy named Mentor in such high regard that he trusts his son's complete education and care to the man. Based on that relationship between a wise teacher and a young learner, the ancient Greek idea of mentoring was born: someone known to be a wise and trustworthy advisor committing to helping the less learned.

Although that idea has been around since the ancient Greeks, networking is a much more twentieth and twenty-first century concept, and since networking is often a great way to identify a mentor, let's discuss that first. I love the networking philosophy of eWomen Network. It is a vast network of women business owners and professionals who are all connected to one another via both a Web site and local chapters in many cities. It is a great way for women to have easy access to one another's skills, talents, knowledge and resources.

Here is this dynamic organization's philosophy of networking, taken directly from its Web site:

> At eWomenNetwork.com our philosophy is that you must first and foremost give to others "first." We believe that by giving and being "other-focused" you create a world of abundance for all. For us, networking is really the art of "giving" and searching for ways to serve the needs of others before focusing on ourselves.

This philosophy must work, because eWomen network is the fastest growing membership-based business-women's network in the country with more than 400,000 members. Founder Sandra Yancey considers the back of your business card your most valuable piece of real estate. It is there that you can write a note or give a referral or other bit of useful advice to a woman you have just met in any networking situation. It really is more about giving than just getting.

Pretty biblical, huh? I lost track counting the number of verses in the Bible that refer to giving—either God giving to us or encouraging us to give to others. Probably the most famous is Acts 20:35 where Jesus is quoted as saying "it is more blessed to give than to receive." That is what both mentoring and networking are all about.

BUILDING BRIDGES

Networking is not just meeting new people in the hopes of finding a mentor. It is about building bridges throughout your professional life that can benefit you and the other person for years to come. I try to make a habit of making notes on people's business cards or in my contacts folder when I first meet them. Are they married? Kids? New in their job or an old pro? If the conversation turns to a particular business challenge, I try to make note of that too and then later share any bit of news or tidbits I think might be useful to my new colleague.

As you can imagine, with my background in human resources, I know that if a new acquaintance is looking for a job or looking to change careers, she wants advice. How can she prepare best for interviewing and how should she get her résumé into shape? How should she decide if she should pursue position A or position B? I generally have a file of articles and tip sheets on certain topics that I can send someone's way when the situation calls for it.

I've also been known to cut out magazine articles or newspaper stories with a particular business slant and send them to a friend who is interested in that subject.

YOU ARE NEVER NOT NETWORKING.

And I keep an in-box folder in my e-mail box full of interesting Web sites and references I may want to share with others later. Networking is about giving and building bridges and nurturing connections that benefit both sides in the future.

In his career transition workshop, John McDorman reminds participants, "You are never not networking." This is so true. I never will forget the time I was consulting with a gentleman who was completely reworking his job search. He had hired me to coach him through the process and help him develop a new set of marketing materials.

While we were sitting at the coffee shop, a recruiter that I knew walked in the door. Believe it or not, he was a sales and marketing recruiter and this man I was working with was a sales and marketing executive! A match made in heaven, I thought. But the fellow I was trying to help didn't have anything with him he could hand the recruiter. Not even a plain old business card with his name, number, and e-mail. Not even a slightly outdated résumé he was able to hand off with the promise to follow up with a spiffy new one later.

Unfortunately, that job seeker didn't take to heart the advice that you are never not networking. He was not prepared to leave a lasting impression, which, in this case, might have led to some job leads. Networking extends well beyond the job search process and into other areas of our professional lives as well.

For those of us who are self-employed, it is obvious that networking can lead to new business opportunities. Nurturing relationships through the art and science of networking is also a critical piece of the mentoring process. Understanding that mentoring must be based on a genuine *relationship* in order to be beneficial to both parties is another critical piece of the puzzle.

A GENUINE RELATIONSHIP

Companies often try to implement "mentoring programs." While the spirit may be right behind such efforts, the results are often less than inspiring. Mentoring relationships happen naturally in most cases. They rarely happen as a result of a spreadsheet-driven program, which may have the hidden objective allowing a management team to "check the box," stating they have implemented something to help people "develop their careers."

Linda Livingstone, the graduate school dean whom we met in chapter one, has an interesting take on mentoring. Even at her level, she still appreciates the value and magic of mentoring. "The most significant mentors in my life are not part of a formal mentoring program, but instead, people who have believed in me and cared about me and whom I respect and trust. It is critical, particularly for women, to seek out these relationships and nurture them over the long run—don't just wait for them to happen. I also believe it is important to have mentors outside of your own organization. This gives you an opportunity for unbiased and fresh perspectives on challenges and opportunities you face."

Whether we take the initiative to develop a mentoring relationship or take advantage of a program within our company, there are some very important things to remember about mentoring so that it provides the greatest amount of benefit.

FORMAL AND INFORMAL

First of all, mentoring relationships can be formal or informal. I'm not referring here to whether or not the mentoring relationship is part of a program, I'm referring more to how it is initiated and what the expectations are from the outset.

In an informal mentoring relationship, there are no specified goals. Whether or not the mentor and mentoree actually achieve anything may be questionable because there has not been agreement about what the relationship is trying to accomplish. The downside here is not only for the individuals in the mentoring relationship, but the business or organization itself does not benefit as much either. The senior leaders of a company are going to be much more open to the idea of mentoring when they see the direct impact it has on business critical skills and the company's strategies.

That is what sets apart a more formalized mentoring process: The mentoring relationship is linked to business objectives, it has established goals, and it outlines measurable outcomes. For instance, let's say I want to develop my ability to analyze financial data and present that data in a confident and knowledgeable fashion to a group of managers. That's a mentoring opportunity for someone in finance, and it directly benefits not only me but the organization as well. It also gives my friend in finance a chance to hone her coaching and communication skills.

You may work in an organization that has a mentoring process, but it is reserved for the top leaders and high-potentials. Or, your business may have a mentoring program that you've just never taken the time to explore. Or perhaps, there is nothing like this in your organization, but the whole idea sounds like it would really benefit your career. You may choose to seek out a mentor inside or outside of your workplace.

For instance, let's say you've been in retail management for a while, running a mom and pop dry cleaners. Your sights are set on moving up—you want to work for a national retail chain with better benefits and greater management opportunities. But you have no idea what skills you need to get there. Time to go mentor shopping—and if you have no idea *where* to find one, go back to point A of this chapter: networking!

WHAT TO LOOK FOR

Who do you look for when you decide a mentor is in order? Well, the number one criteria for a mentor should be an individual you respect, a person with the utmost integrity. If it is someone you don't know, perhaps someone you met through a networking situation or referred by Uncle Jim's third cousin Susie from down the street, do your research to make sure the potential mentor has a stellar reputation. You obviously don't want to latch onto someone who ends up in the slammer on a fraud conviction or gets fired for falsifying expense reports.

The second thing to look for is an individual who is respected by those in authority. Who gets asked to be present at meetings when the head honchos come in from headquarters for a visit? Who gets scheduled to work the day shift when the regional manager is coming to town? Maybe you seek out a person who holds an office in the local chapter of your particular professional association.

Finally, a mentor should possess unique knowledge and expertise not only in the specific field or skill in which you need to develop, but she should have overall street smarts too—be business savvy and have organizational acumen and that important political shrewdness we discussed earlier. Your mentor is there to help you not just to grow your skills but also possibly to help you navigate tricky situations. Make sure she's really got the expertise to help.

A CERTAIN AMOUNT OF CHEMISTRY IS NECESSARY FOR AN EFFECTIVE MENTORING RELATIONSHIP.

In addition to the business skills and credibility, there is a certain amount of chemistry necessary for an effective mentoring relationship. Open and honest communication is obviously critical. So are empathy and the ability to be non-judgmental. These are all characteristics of the relationship you should discuss at the onset, so you can know for sure how committed a person is to these operating principles.

What's the absolutely positively *most* essential aspect to finding a mentor? Prayer! Believers have the distinct advantage of the Holy Spirit to lead us to someone with whom we can develop a mutually beneficial relationship. Jesus calls the Holy Spirit our counselor (John 14:16). We should definitely rely on that heavenly counselor to direct us to the person who will be our best career counselor.

MEET SABRINA O'MALONE

Sabrina O'Malone is the former Mrs. New Jersey, founder of www.workingmom.com, an online ministry to those juggling motherhood and career and author of *Prayers for the Working Mom.* She is the mother of three young children and she spent more than 10 years working full-time as a pharmaceutical sales representative. Throughout her career, she has relied on mentors for both professional and spiritual growth. Sabrina not only believes in the power of prayer to *find* a mentor, but advises women to initiate a mentoring relationship by asking the potential mentor to pray *for* you.

"If you feel God is leading you to someone, a 'big girl' in the faith that you know can mentor you, then ask her to pray for you." Sabrina has seen this open doors to ongoing mentoring relationships as the "pray-er" follows up with the "prayee." "When you find that woman whom you know has pearls of wisdom to share with you, and you want to sit at her feet and learn, prayer is the first step."

After you have set your sights on someone you'd like to mentor you, you need to carefully think through what you hope to get out of the relationship, as well as what you can give. Don't approach a busy colleague with the enthusiasm of a golden retriever puppy without a plan. "Hi! I wanna be your new best friend!" Do that, and watch the person run the other way!

How do you make a mentoring plan? First, align it with the overall goals of your company and/or career. Is the company goal this quarter to open new markets or launch a new product? Is it to stem turnover and build employee morale? Or following our earlier example, is the goal to help you develop a short-term plan to make a long-term career move? If you can link what you hope to accomplish in the mentoring relationship to broader strategies in the business or in your career, it helps establish the relationship on firm footing from the get go.

FOR A SUCCESSFUL MENTORING RELATIONSHIP, MEASURABLE GOALS SHOULD BE ESTABLISHED.

A successful mentoring relationship should have some measurable goals. Perhaps you want to develop a certain skill or hone one of your strengths to compensate for your weakness. Let's say you really want to improve your presentation skills, for instance. You choose a mentor who's a crackerjack presenter and always wows the management team with her eloquence, humor, and fact-based presentations. She agrees to coach you and help you rehearse for the next big meeting.

How will you measure the results? Well, if you have a performance plan, this developmental objective might already be there. If not, then develop some ways to chart your progress in this particular skill. Maybe you and your mentor check with the team after your presentations to get feedback for you. Find a book on effective presentations, create your own evaluation form, and sit down together to check your progress.

ENDING THE RELATIONSHIP

In addition to measurable goals, there needs to be agreement that at any time, either the mentor or mentoree can end the relationship. Mentors are like old boyfriends; you have to know when to let them go. They change, you change, and the connection is no longer of mutual benefit. Both the mentor and the mentoree have to be able to end the formal mentoring aspect of relationship, recognizing with no hurt feelings that the mentoring has served its purpose. (Don't get carried away now—this doesn't mean you can't go to lunch occasionally or visit when the opportunity arises—it just means that you've stopped formally meeting with a specific purpose in mind.)

In essence, this is what you wanted to happen in the first place—you learn yourself out of a particular mentoring relationship in order to move on to the next characteristic or competency you want to develop. You have refined or developed the skills you were seeking to develop, and the mentor can watch her prodigy progress to other challenges with pride.

While this sounds like a love 'em and leave 'em experience, in reality what I'm suggesting is far from it. All relationships progress through cycles. If I meet regularly with someone for a time because I'm trying to develop my ability to think strategically, and I prove myself a few times in that area, then my regular meetings may turn into occasional e-mails to celebrate successes or seek feedback and advice. At some point after that you realize, "Hey, I can be a mentor too!"

MENTORS BENEFIT, TOO!

Let's explore in more depth how mentoring benefits the mentor. Remember our earlier premise? That this is just as much about giving as getting? Well, mentors gain some interesting things in the process of taking someone under their wing. If the mentor is within your organization, then she will learn more about the company by getting to know someone who does something different from her.

If she's someone outside your company, then she has the advantage of learning about another business and how it works. In the course of discussing policies, procedures, and processes that differ, the mentor develops a broader perspective of how her field operates.

In addition, the mentor learns things from the mentoree's background and history that can be used in their own professional and personal development. The mentor develops the ability to effectively communicate success strategies and help someone develop specific skills and competencies. If the mentor is already a people manager, then mentoring someone else can be a refresher on good coaching skills. Familiarity breeds contempt and all that—there's nothing like trying to communicate to someone *new* what you try to communicate to the same old faces day after day. A mentoring relationship can really push a manager outside her comfort zone when it comes to communicating effectively with people about specific skills and competencies.

Finally, there is one last advantage for the mentor: It is satisfying to share our expertise with others. Admit it—we all like to talk about ourselves, and areas where we think we excel. If you want to test my theory, approach your manager this week and ask, "Can you tell me about a time you solved a particularly difficult problem here at the office? How did you do it?" Watch those eyes light up and listen to the stories start to flow!

BIBLE MENTORS

Mentoring is a biblical concept. Think of all the early leaders of the New Testament church who had their mentor/mentoree relationships. In fact, two of our New Testament books are based on the mentoring relationship between the apostle Paul and his protégé Timothy. Unfortunately for those guys, they didn't have e-mail and cell phones. Fortunately for us, though, we're left with two epistles that reveal the true heart of the mentoring relationship.

In both books, Paul opens by calling Timothy his dear son. Now while I don't recommend that you require a mentor to address you as a "dear daughter" or, on the flip side, address your mentoree with such intimate language, what is conveyed here is genuine care and concern for the individual. That is critically important in any mentoring relationship. What follows in Paul's two instruction books to Timothy is mentoring at its finest: specific, relevant training and words of wisdom directly related to Timothy's task at hand—preaching and teaching and building churches in Ephesus and Asia Minor.

The Old Testament shows us examples of mentoring too. Moses certainly mentored Joshua during years of wilderness wandering and battles. In Exodus 17 we first meet the young man Joshua, who is called an aide to Moses throughout Scripture. The wise man of God and leader of His chosen people certainly had many opportunities to mentor this young man and must have been proud of his protégé when, in Deuteronomy 31, he commissions him as the one who will lead the people into the Promised Land and many new adventures.

It was undoubtedly a bittersweet moment. Because of his sin, Moses would not see the land flowing with milk and honey, but this man Joshua, who had stood by him since his youth, was now ready to take the leadership role God had ordained long ago. "Be strong and courageous…" are Moses' words in Deuteronomy 31:7. Sometimes, that may be all we need to hear from our mentors, "Be strong and courageous!"

While the topics of our mentoring relationships may never equal the weightiness of Paul and Timothy's challenges in building the early church, or Moses and Joshua's challenges of leading God's chosen people, they are nonetheless opportunities to build genuine relationships. Certainly the ultimate example of mentoring in Scripture is the example of Jesus and His disciples.

THE ULTIMATE EXAMPLE OF MENTORING IS JESUS AND HIS DISCIPLES.

Jesus picked out a dozen men, and then mentored them more or less continually for the next three years. The relationship between Jesus and those original twelve is a story of living out life to its fullest, but it's also a story of daily-ness: They traveled, they ate, they talked, they asked questions, they debated and experienced life-changing adventure. Most important to those mentoree disciples, though, they learned by example.

MENTORING FOR SPIRITUAL GROWTH

We see from Scripture that mentoring is a remarkably effective way to grow. While the topic of this book is professional growth, we'd be missing out on something big if we failed to mention the role of mentoring in our spiritual growth. Consider the book of Titus, a letter Paul wrote to one of his other mentorees, the Gentile convert of the same name. It's one of those books you probably have to use the table of contents to find. It is just a few pages hidden between 2 Timothy and that other oft-overlooked letter to Philemon.

In Titus 2:3–5, there is specific instruction for older women to teach younger women important lessons for life. This passage, which validates the notion of the wiser teaching and guiding the younger, is the basis for many women's ministries' mentoring programs in churches across the world.

Linda Livingstone again advises us on the link between faith, work, and mentoring. "Being a woman of faith in the workplace presents many unique challenges and opportunities, particularly as you work with those who have different values. Because of this, I really encourage women to include among their mentors one or more people who understand and support their faith commitment. These individuals can help keep you grounded in your faith and true to your values even in difficult situations."

As I look back on my own life, I can remember different people who have mentored me in various areas of my personal, professional, and spiritual life. Some of them I still rely on today. Others I've lost touch with, but I remember the impact they had on my life or career during a particularly impressionable time.

The reflection causes me to stop and think of my interactions with those just starting out, or those in career transition. What can I offer? How can I help? What bit of wisdom, learned from my own hard knocks, can I impart? What content expertise do I possess that can help someone at the beginning stage of her career?

You see, the greatest value of having mentors at various stages of your career is being able to be a mentor to others someday. You will be able to look at their career, watch their talent grow, and know you had some bit of impact on their success.

And remember that anyone can be a mentor. Regardless of your position or role—sales clerk to sales operations vice president—you have something of value to teach someone. Stop and think about it through a stoplight or two, and you'll realize that you too have the power to impart the magic of mentoring.

LESSONS AT WORK

Think:

• What skills and competencies do you observe in others that you know you need to develop yourself?

• Who do you admire at work, and why? Does that individual possess talent or demonstrate a level of business savvy that you know would benefit your career and your company?

- If a career change is on the horizon, or if you are just starting out, who do you know in your field who can mentor you as you make a transition?
- How can a mentoring relationship benefit not only you, but your business? What are your company's strategic objectives right now? Maybe it is simply to continue ramping up sales, but how can seeking a mentor for yourself help you do your part more effectively?
- As you consider embarking on a mentoring relationship, what are specific things you would like to achieve? What behaviors or skills would you desire to change or enhance as a result of your mentoring relationship? Can you state those in measurable terms, like increased sales volume or number of recovered customers?
- Think through how you will "sell" the mentoring relationship to your prospective mentor. How can you explain, in terminology that resonates within your business, the mutually beneficial results of mentoring?
- What if the roles are reversed? What unique skills do you possess that can benefit a mentoree? How can you use your knowledge and experience to benefit others?

Do:

- Make a plan and write it down. Commit to paper what a successful mentoring relationship will look like.
- Visit with your manager or human resources department and find out if there is a mentoring program in your company that you can take advantage of. If not, present your business case and demonstrate to your manager why this is a worthwhile idea. (Make sure she knows you are not trying to *replace* her!)

- Take a look at www.marketplaceleaders.org. This organization is committed to enriching believers at work and it offers a mentoring membership to help with a variety of both career and faith development issues. The Marketplace Mentor is an affordable program for just about anyone.

CHAPTER SIX

Integrity Intensified

LESSON #6
THERE'S NO SUCH THING AS TOO MUCH INTEGRITY.

"Real integrity is doing the right thing, knowing that nobody is going to know whether you did it or not."
—Oprah Winfrey

W e don't have to scan far into today's headlines to see that integrity is lacking in today's marketplace. Scandals of fraud and mismanagement have rocked nearly every industry, affecting both employees and shareholders, often with disastrous results. In my own career, I have seen powerful men and women fall from atop golden career ladders because they made wrong choices in the integrity department. I even got a negative mark in the integrity category on a performance review once. It knocked the wind out of my sails for sure! I will tell you more about it later.

Linda Livingstone mentions that ethics programs conducted for MBA students sometimes include guest speakers who have been convicted of and served time for white-collar crimes. "According to some of these individuals, seemingly insignificant decisions ultimately led them to make more significant decisions that resulted in going down a far different road than they ever thought they would go. It is the apparently insignificant decisions we make each day that shape our character and prepare us for how we will respond when more important and challenging choices come our way."

We would probably be surprised at the number of people crossing our daily paths who have succumbed to major ethical lapses. It is interesting that our society seems to have a high degree of tolerance for those who have made mistakes in the ethics and integrity department. Martha Stewart did her jail time but her stock jumped up 6 percent the night before her prison release. The pundits are currently arguing how quick and effective her turnaround will be, but most agree she'll eventually return to her status as the primo decorator, gardener, and cookie baker that she has always been.

Many of us watched *Catch Me if You Can* with a mix of amusement and awe. Steven Spielberg's 2002 movie starred Leonardo DiCaprio and Tom Hanks. It was a movie based on the life of Frank Abagnale Jr, who made a life out of impersonating various professionals and defrauding banks. After being convicted and serving his time, he became a security consultant to the same types of companies he used to scam. He has his own Web site and purports to be one of the world's most respected authorities on the subjects of forgery, embezzlement, and secure documents. He even lectures at the FBI Academy! How's that for a story of redemption?

AN INTEGRITY-CHALLENGED WORLD

In spite of our society's occasional willingness to forgive and the stories of individuals who have seemed to demonstrate that crime *does* pay, most of the time shortcomings in the integrity department result in ruined careers and demolished lives. How are we as believers in business to think about integrity? Although we may have never been tempted to cook the books or commit insider trading, are there areas we still need to explore in the integrity-challenged world in which we operate today?

I say yes, definitely. Let's consider one of Jesus' first teachings, the Sermon on the Mount, and you'll see why. I usually quote from the New International Version, but in this case, I'm going to use *The Message* with a few of my own thoughts inserted as well. I love how this version makes Jesus' words come to life in order to demonstrate way above-board behavior. Here it is, Matthew 5:21–28:

> "You're familiar with the command to the ancients, 'Do not murder.' I'm telling you that anyone who is so much as angry with a brother or sister is guilty of murder. Carelessly call a brother 'idiot!' and you just might find yourself hauled into court. [Boy, is that true in our litigious society or what?] Thoughtlessly yell 'stupid!' at a sister and you are on the brink of hellfire. The simple moral fact is that words kill.
>
> "This is how I want you to conduct yourself in these matters. If you enter your place of worship and, about to make an offering, you suddenly remember a grudge a friend has against you, abandon your offering, leave immediately, go to this friend and make things right. Then and only then, come back and work things out with God.
>
> "Or say you're out on the street [or at the office] and an old enemy accosts you. Don't lose a minute. Make the first move; make things right with him. After all, if you leave the first move to him, knowing his track record, you're likely to end up in court, maybe even jail. If that happens, you won't get out without a stiff fine.
>
> "You know the next commandment pretty well, too: 'Don't go to bed with another's spouse.' But don't think you've preserved your virtue simply by staying out of bed. Your heart can be corrupted by lust even quicker than your body [especially when that cute guy from accounting walks past your door]. Those leering looks you think nobody notices—they also corrupt."

Jesus continues His teaching with other examples of how believers are supposed to behave very differently from those who do not know God. We are definitely called to a higher standard. I don't think we are to be all high and mighty and pompously prudish, but these teachings have huge implications for us in the integrity department when it comes to work and other facets of our lives.

I would like to address three areas in the subject of integrity. In my experience, they are three of the areas in which women struggle the most. I want us to carefully consider integrity in speech, image, and what I will refer to as our MO: modus operandi—how we function, not necessarily what we do but how we do it. This applies to us regardless of what we do for a living, regardless of our position, and regardless of how far along we are in our careers.

Before we launch, I also want to make one more point about integrity, especially before you get your defenses up. Integrity isn't just about *not doing the wrong things*. (Grammarians, I realize that is a double negative. Sorry.) Integrity also has to do with doing the right thing to an even greater degree. Let's start with our speech (yikes!) and you'll see what I mean.

INTEGRITY IN OUR SPEECH

There's plenty in the Bible to remind us that our speech has an intensity of power and purpose that few of us ever really get our arms around, or our lips around as the case may be. James 3:5–10 is probably the most famous of all those verses:

> "Likewise the tongue is a small part of the body, but it makes great boasts. Consider what a great forest is set on

fire by a small spark. The tongue also is a fire, a world of evil among the parts of the body. It corrupts the whole person, sets the whole course of his life on fire, and is itself set on fire by hell. All kinds of animals, birds, reptiles and creatures of the sea are being tamed and have been tamed by man, but no man can tame the tongue. It is a restless evil, full of deadly poison. With the tongue we praise our Lord and Father, and with it we curse men, who have been made in God's likeness. Out of the same mouth come praise and cursing. My brothers, this should not be."

The Proverbs 31 woman had evidently overcome in this area: "She speaks in wisdom and faithful instruction is on her tongue," according to verse 26. Vicki Courtney, in her fabulous book *The Virtuous Woman,* devotes a whole section to this subject and this verse. I love the chapter title: "If you can't say something nice...." I could fill a whole book with situations at work and life in general in which I did not speak in wisdom and later regretted it. Several significant areas come to mind when we're talking about the tongue: gossip, inappropriate talk, response to insults, and managing conflict.

GOSSIP

It is so easy to fall into the gossip trap. Even as Christian women, who are supposed to be so sweet and kind, we are easily tempted to jump into discussions about the latest scoop on the girl in operations or the grumpy old lady in the home office. We sometimes even use "prayer requests" as an excuse to talk about the personal crisis in someone's life instead of just leaving it at "Pray for Bill and Sally—God knows what they need."

I find myself wrestling with this as a mother too. Of course, I want to stay on top of what is going on with the teens my son hangs out with at school and the periphery of friends and acquaintances he has there, but sometimes his outlandish reports and third-person stories can sound like gossip instead of what they start out as: "Mom, we need to pray for...." I want to encourage him to share with me what is happening and what he thinks about it, but to help him realize the difference between processing the personal growth pangs of adolescence and outright gossip.

At work, the most successful strategy to deal with gushing gossip is to walk away. It doesn't do us much good to just keep our mouths shut but then sit there at the lunch table and listen to all the dirt being dished out. We can change the subject as soon as it is feasible or finish what we are doing and move on.

Not participating in juicy gossip sessions builds trust between our co-workers and us. If Carol in sales has been thinking about sharing a personal problem with you because she knows you are a person of faith, she's much more likely to bring you into her confidence if she sees you back away from the gossip sessions by the soda machine.

INAPPROPRIATE TALK

The next area regarding our speech that we should consider has to do with inappropriate talk. Here is where I struggle. I don't mean cussing like a sailor but rather letting my speech slip into clever jabs or funny insults that get a laugh but do little to build up a person or really help the situation.

Another related phenomenon I observed occurred shortly after all the sexual discrimination laws were passed years ago. The people in human resources, tasked with training everyone on what was now appropriate and inappropriate, the very folks trying to enforce this new set of standards, became the greatest source for inappropriate, sexually related humor. Sure, sometimes it is very hard not to laugh and chime in with something we were sent over e-mail or heard in another meeting, but we have to remember our calling to be above reproach.

Different company cultures have different levels of what is acceptable. Personal jab fests and "Yo' mamma is so ugly..." joke contests may be de rigueur in your warehouse, but that doesn't make these conversations right. They may be *funny*, but not *right*! My advice is to tread cautiously here and try to keep your speech pure while walking the fine line to not be prudish or appear stuck up or self-righteous. If nothing else, in the highly litigious society in which we live, you may keep yourself out of a difficult employee relations situation that degenerates into a "he said/she said" battle or something even worse.

RESPONSE TO INSULTS

Closely linked to this idea is how we respond to insult or personal injury. When we have been slighted, it is easy to jump into a defensive mode and launch into the offending person with a barrage of angrily fueled insults. Remember the old trick of counting to ten before we say something—good advice here. A couple of deep breaths and a quickly muttered prayer can make the difference between an all-out conflict and a brief encounter that fades away.

When a conflict arises and hurtful words begin to bubble to the surface, we have two choices, and I strongly suggest relying on the Holy Spirit to determine which path to take.

We can either calmly confront the offender with a fact-based, personal statement like, "You know, Sue, that comment you made in yesterday's meeting really hurt my feelings. I want to have positive working relationships with all my colleagues, so I wanted you to know how I feel." Then leave it at that. Most times, people like Sue will apologize.

The other option is to walk away from the insult and leave it alone. It's in God's hands. Deuteronomy 32:35 clearly illustrates God's protective heart toward His people: "It is mine to avenge; I will repay. In due time their foot will slip; their day of disaster is near and their doom rushes upon them." It might be tempting to write this verse on a sticky note and leave it on mean ol' Sue's desk, but no need. As I've said before, truth will prevail. If Sue does not clean up her interpersonal act, sooner or later her career will take a different tack, and those who choose to be kind in the face of conflict and insult will more likely be the ones who prevail.

MANAGING CONFLICT

Let's talk a little more about quarrels and how we handle those with a heart and mouth full of integrity. When an occasional insult from a co-worker has tumbled down the mountain into an ongoing conflict, all sorts of things can start to happen. One, we might find ourselves tempted to gossip about the grouchy woman who is making our work lives miserable right now. Or we may be tempted to hurl insults her way. In short, our tongues can take off without our brains when a disagreement has turned into an ongoing eruption of emotional engagement.

It's time for heartfelt prayer once again. The Lord promises to give us wisdom, and nowhere is wisdom more necessary than in difficult relationships. How we handle a conflict says volumes about what we believe. In addition to prayer, you probably have some additional options, depending on your company. Asking your manager to help mediate and solve a problem with a coworker can be a good route to repairing a relationship.

HOW WE HANDLE A CONFLICT SAYS VOLUMES ABOUT WHAT WE BELIEVE.

Of course, if the manager is the problem, then you may have to take advantage of your company's "open door" policy that may look something like going over your manager's head with no fear of reprisal. You may have a mediation program, human resources teams who are available to help with conflict, or an ombudsman. Find out what options are available to solve work-related conflict. Remember, you are there to work! You are paid a salary to achieve business objectives. If you take the high road and initiate the resolution of a conflict that is distracting you from your work, you'll be seen as someone with high integrity and a commitment to the business. People who respond well in the face of conflict are valuable commodities to productivity-minded management teams.

One last word about our words. Okay, maybe more than one. Integrity of speech is not just about what we *don't* say; it's about what we *do* say. We can season our words with principles from Scripture and make a difference in how our daily lives are lived out among our co-workers. We can do the right thing even righter.

In her study *Believing God*, Beth Moore writes: "When Christ empowered his disciples to speak under his authority and produce certain results, he treated the tongue as an instrument. . . . The Holy Spirit infuses power through the instrument. ... When we believe and speak, the Holy Spirit can use our tongues as instruments or vessels of supernatural power and can bring about stunning results."

Beth refers to a powerful Scripture in 2 Corinthians 4:13. Read it with new eyes and ears—hear what it says to us about life at work: "It is written, 'I believed; therefore I have spoken.' With that same spirit of faith we also believe and therefore speak because we know that the one who raised the Lord Jesus from the dead will also raise us with Jesus and present us with you in his presence." If we speak the words we believe based on what we believe, we speak with power and we speak the presence of God into our marketplace.

Joyce Meyer, in her bestselling book, *Me and My Big Mouth,* discusses in depth this powerful, positive impact our words can have. In fact, the subtitle, "the answer is right under your nose" indicates that the influential power wrought by our words is often the key to handling a difficult situation.

In contrast, my mother used to have a copy of a book titled *Winning Through Intimidation*. The concept of winning by backing someone into a corner and scaring her to death does not reflect the overwhelming love God has for people. When we choose to "season our words with salt" and consciously use scripturally inspired words (not necessarily verbatim), we convey not just a love and grace that is uncommon in today's frenetic world, but we also demonstrate the relevance of those ancient principles to modern reality.

This is not about spouting the King James each time you stand up in a meeting. This is not about preaching. You haven't knocked someone over the head with a Bible, you're just sharing a bit of your personal story, a bit of your faith, a bit of your heart. That's what people respond to. That's how we take the message of God's love to the workplace with integrity.

INTEGRITY OF IMAGE

Now this only works when our image is consistent with our words. Let's say we have tamed the temptation to gossip, we've got our conflict management skills honed to an art, and we haven't told a dirty joke since our last slumber party in ninth grade. Check all those boxes. In addition to those, though, our image also says volumes about what we believe, who we are, and how we live out integrity in the workplace.

Now, before you check the limit on your credit card and run out to buy a new wardrobe, hear me out. I'm not just talking about how we dress, although dressing for success has great merit. I am talking about the whole package: how we present ourselves not just physically but also through our interactions in the workplace. Paying attention to the details can convey our integrity.

MEET KAREN PORTER

Karen Porter is the vice president of international marketing at American Rice, Inc. Have you ever wondered who travels the world selling rice grown in the U.S.A.? Well, it's your new friend, Karen Porter, and she sells *lots* of rice. Somehow, she also has time to lead Bible studies, write books, and speak words of encouragement to women's groups. Here are this executive's words of encouragement for us regarding integrity and image:

> When you walk in that office every morning, make sure that you radiate a positive image. From what you wear to the way you carry your head, exude confidence, discernment, and willingness to work. When the executives look around for someone to lead the next project team, your professional image will be remembered.

When I refer to image I do include how we dress. I'm all for using my femininity in a winsome way to endear myself to people. The days of stuffy blue business suits have finally given way to business wear for a woman that does not look like a military uniform (hallelujah!). That said, though, I can't spout stuff that sounds like Scripture one day and wear a cleavage-revealing blouse and too-short skirt the next. It is important to consider our appearance and dress appropriately for our jobs (whether that is business suits or blue jeans and tennis shoes). With the prevalence of lingerie-on-the-outside fashions today, some of which are really cute, this can be a challenge. We have to carefully consider how to be stylish and still appropriate at the same time.

MEET JILL KRIEGER SWANSON

Jill Krieger Swanson is a certified image consultant with more than 25 years of experience and training in the color and fashion industry. She motivates women to exude an outer confidence that powerfully expresses their inner qualities. Recognizing that professionals lead busy lives, she helps clients achieve a put-together look to suit their individual jobs and resources. She also believes in the connection between image and integrity.

"I often remind my clients that when you first meet a person, what is remembered about you is 90 percent what you look like and 10 percent what you say," remarks Jill. "If you walk out the door in the morning and look polished, put together and professional then you become that. Your dress affects your image from the inside out. If you look dowdy or frumpy you tend to take on that persona during the day and your self-confidence plummets."

I once saw Jill do a hilarious and yet hard-hitting presentation on image. I was at a conference. The next thing on the agenda was a session on portraying a professional image. I glanced behind me, and sitting at the back table was the goofiest looking lady I'd seen in quite a while. I don't mean to sound mean, but this woman really was fashion-challenged. Her hair was in a tight bun, her glasses were left over from the how-big-can-your-plastic-frames-be era, and she was wearing a bad suit with a big-bowed blouse.

Thank the Lord she is going to hear the next speaker, I thought. *This woman needs a serious update.* Well, I was horrified when frump-girl took the podium twenty minutes later. I thought the conference organizers, in whom I normally have complete confidence, had lost their collective minds.

But then there before our eyes, frump-girl began to talk about image and success and professionalism and, as she talked, she transformed her whole look. The eyeglasses were removed, the hair came down into gorgeous, wavy locks, and the suit was peeled off thanks to velcroed back seams to reveal a stylish and polished outfit underneath. It was a riot. She made her point quite well.

"When I do that presentation, it really hits home that what you wear affects who you are," Jill says. "I am a very confident person, but when I walk out in my frump-girl costume, it is very hard to convey that."

In her book *Simply Beautiful Inside and Out,* Jill reminds us that if we are to be salt and light in a world where people judge by outward appearances, then we may need to move forward to make some changes in our appearance. If we embrace an outer image that dates us, people think our ideas and opinions are dated as well.

OUR IMAGE HAS IMPACT ON OUR INTEGRITY IN THE WORKPLACE.

If a woman came to your door offering expertise on interior decorating dressed in a frumpy polyester suit, bouffant hairdo, and oversized glasses, would you be willing to hire her to redesign your domain? Probably not. What if she wanted to share her spiritual beliefs? Again, no way. Now imagine that same woman with an updated hairstyle and glasses and dressed in a structured black suit with a crisp white blouse. Suddenly she has our attention and respect.

Hey, it may not be right. Perhaps we should totally ignore what people look like, but few of us do. For that reason, our image has impact on our integrity in the workplace. This extends beyond what we wear. When we send out e-mails or other written communications full of typographical errors, we convey a carelessness that does not reflect the scriptural command to do all things excellently. When we put together a presentation for our manager and fail to proofread it carefully, we risk damaging not only our reputation but hers too.

I will never forget the time I developed a quarterly slide show for Michael Dell. It was in the early days of the company when everyone could still crowd into conference rooms across our sprawling campuses and, throughout the course of the day, our CEO could make the rounds and give us an update on how we were doing in our quest to be number one. The theme of this particular presentation was something about "surprise" and, to my surprise; I had been misspelling that little two-syllable word all my life. I left out the first "r."

This was in the days before Bill Gates and his software developers made it virtually impossible for us to misspell words. I didn't realize what had happened until halfway through the day when I found myself under the ominous glare of the CEO's powerful administrative assistant. She politely but firmly made sure I realized how important it was to get the leader's slides right. She didn't use the scriptural command, "Do all things excellently," but I certainly got the message. That instance brought home the lesson that both my image and the image of those I work for can be affected by lapses in my integrity—even when it's something as unintended as a misspelling.

In a world where second best will often do, we can truly set ourselves apart by portraying an image of professionalism and excellence. My mother used to tell me to dress and act like those a step ahead of me on the career ladder. That's not a bad idea. Beyond dress, though, and beyond making sure we don't mistake "there" for "their," our integrity is also impacted by our MO: our modus operandi. (You didn't know I spoke Latin, huh? Watch this, now I'm going to throw in some French!)

MODUS OPERANDI PAR EXCELLENCE

Modus operandi is a Latin phrase, approximately translated as "mode of operation," and commonly used to describe someone's habits. Our habits at work, how we operate not just what we do, say a great deal about our integrity. Consider these aspects of our days in the marketplace and you will see what I mean:

• Do I always arrive rushing in or late for my shift or for meetings, or do I get there in time to relax and prepare for what lies ahead?

• Do I plan out my day the afternoon before so I am certain I'm ready for any deadlines, conference calls, or encounters I know I will have the following day?

• Do I complete my projects on time and under budget, to the best of my ability?

• How do I respond when I don't know the answer to a question? Do I make something up or say, "I need to get back to you," and then really follow up?

- Do I behave consistently with my company's culture? (In some companies it is better to plow ahead and seek forgiveness later if necessary—the classic, "just do it" approach. In other workplaces, it is essential to ask permission before launching into something.)

The list could go on and on. These are just a few of the basic work habits that can convey our commitment to excellence in all things and therefore a level of integrity that is too often missing in the workplace today. These are ways we put feet on our faith and at the same time solidify our standing as a valuable employee.

I mentioned earlier that I got a low mark once in the integrity department on a performance review. I was horrified. After all, I'm a Christian! I never stole anything from my business, never falsified anything, did what I was supposed to do, and overall had a stellar reputation, I thought. What was this about?

When my manager and I dug into the definition of integrity in our performance management system, there was an interesting line: It had to do with *grandstanding*. Grandstanding means to act so as to impress. In the integrity category, this can convey that we are only out for ourselves. Well, in my situation, I had been through so many reorganizations and management changes, I felt a need to make sure everyone knew how competent I was. It came across the wrong way, though. Instead of letting my actions and accomplishments speak for themselves, I had tooted my own horn a few too many times.

It was time to eat a slice of humble pie.

I daresay I'm not the only working woman who has struggled with grandstanding. Women working in an industry or a field dominated by men may feel a need to implement a personal public relations campaign, especially if trying to move forward in their career. Warning: Proceed with caution. Owning our own careers and making a plan to move ahead does not mean grandstanding.

In 2 Timothy 2:14–16, we are given some advice on how we should present ourselves, and it isn't hard to see how this applies to our work life. Paul writes, "Warn them before God against quarreling about words; it is of no value, and only ruins those who listen. Do your best to present yourself to God as one approved, a workman who does not need to be ashamed and who correctly handles the word of truth. Avoid godless chatter, because those who indulge in it will become more and more ungodly."

We are called to present ourselves to God as workmen—that means we are doing our work. Our actions speak for themselves. Yes, we have earth-bound managers and roles and responsibilities, and we should do our work with pride and excellence. But ultimately, we are presenting our work to the Lord. We rely on His strength and timing, and we should definitely avoid godless chatter, especially if it is about us! Though the title may be tantalizing, the last thing we want to do is talk ourselves into a position or a set of responsibilities that we are not really qualified to handle. That's grandstanding that leads to not only a huge lapse of integrity, but career disaster as well!

MEET JANE JARRELL

Jane Jarrell, the author of 14 books and coauthor of 20, is a charter member of the MOPS International Speakers bureau, sought-after speaker, and radio and television guest who speaks on leadership, lifestyle balance, and numerous topics for mothers. She is president of High-heels and Homelife, a ministry to working mothers. After successful careers with Neiman Marcus and Southern Living, she knows a thing or two about integrity and work.

"Ultimately our employer is the Lord," Jane reminds us. "It is easy to fall into comparison and pride in the workplace and that radically affects our integrity." Jane does not believe that competition and striving to get ahead in our careers is all bad, but we must be cautious. "Sometimes we become so driven, so 'type A,' that we do things we wouldn't normally do. That competitiveness to get ahead can become sinful." For Jane, prayer is the key to overcoming this struggle. "When I sense myself getting caught in this competition trap, I really have to remind myself of my mission. Again, my employer is the Lord."

It was a lesson I learned during that performance review and one I am sure I will learn over and over again. Balancing the need to convey what we are capable of and yet not becoming prideful and obnoxiously arrogant requires heavenly wisdom and a commitment to integrity.

Another aspect of our MO at work that deserves some attention is the need to persevere. This is especially important when we are ready to just give up. Whether the challenge is changing jobs, finding a new job, finishing a difficult project, resolving a conflict, or switching to a new field, sometimes the race is long and hard and we are tempted to quit the race in the middle of the race track.

Perseverance and strength in the face of ongoing struggle is a dramatic way to display our integrity to a world that is quick to throw in the towel. Karol Ladd is the best-selling author of 15 books, including *The Power of a Positive Wife* and *The Power of a Positive Mom*. In *The Power of a Positive Woman*, Karol concludes with the challenging chapter, "Press On!" She reminds us of some stories many of us have heard before. Think about these the next time you are tempted to jeopardize your integrity by giving up at work:

• Michael Jordan was cut from his high school basketball team.
• Albert Einstein's Ph.D. dissertation was rejected.
• Henry Ford went bankrupt twice during his first three years in the automotive business.
• And one that involves an author near to every mother's heart: Dr. Seuss's first children's book was rejected by 23 publishers. (Say it with me, "One fish two fish red fish blue fish….")

Karol goes on to write that though these people faced discouragement, "they did not lose heart….We need to keep our eyes on the big, eternal picture and stop sweating the small stuff." Indeed, a heavenly bird's-eye view of life and work helps us keep our ambition and therefore our integrity in check. We don't need to rush God's plan for our careers. He's had it mapped out from day one of eternity.

Luci Swindoll has some fabulous advice on this topic: "We think we have to be super mom/employee/ volunteer but that's not possible. We are called to simply do the next thing God's asked us to do and not leap over tall buildings, not take care of the whole world." Luci reminds us that when we take on too much, everything suffers, and that impacts our integrity. "Meet your deadlines. Ask questions to alleviate the pain of assumption. And remember, there is no substitute for love and grace and caring for people in the workplace." Those behaviors certainly add up to an image of integrity in a marketplace that needs all the love, grace, and care that it can get!

Finally, we have one last topic in our discussion of integrity. If you've read this chapter and thought, *Well, fine, but I can only tackle one of these targets at a time,* then this is probably the one to start with. It begins with one of the first things that your mother probably taught you.

THE GOLDEN RULE OF INTEGRITY

"Do unto others as you would have them do unto you." It's a phrase many of us have heard since we were watching Sesame Street and eating peanut butter directly from the jar. (Some of you still do, admit it.) It is still relevant today and in fact has been augmented by other similar thoughts and phrases like, "Everything I need to know I learned in kindergarten (or from my dog or my cat, etc.)" and "Practice random acts of kindness and beauty."

We've been bombarded lately with simple messages of great truth that are easily forgotten in our frenetically busy society. We miss moments of grandeur in our lives and the lives of others because we're too busy. We have forgotten how to play with each other and enjoy one another's company even at work. We've heard that it takes more muscles to frown than it does to smile.

Unfortunately, our response has been to avoid eye contact altogether.

Making the golden rule part of our modus operandi is the fastest way to demonstrate our integrity at work and in the workplace. It is also the primary way we demonstrate the love of God to others.

When I am pleasant to the lady checking out my groceries, she's more likely to be nice to her kids when she gets home from a tough job on her feet all day. When I smile to the tollbooth agent, he's more likely to smile at the driver of the next car zipping by. When I look my manager in the eye, smile, and say "good morning," it is more likely to be just that—a good morning.

We sometimes equate kindness with weakness, or we assume that one can't be kind and be competitive, or be nice and relentlessly focused on the business's goals at the same time. But we can treat others as we want to be treated and still make tough business decisions! We'll just do it more humanely.

It takes less effort and less energy to see the best in people, overlook small offenses, and be kind. I discovered that this particular commitment to integrity paid off for me in two ways. First, I could leave any organization or project with my head held high knowing I had treated others well. Second, I have a Rolodex full of business cards from former and current colleagues whom I can contact at any time.

When we talk about the Golden Rule, especially as it relates to work, there is one thing to remember. Some people in our worlds, in spite of our acts of kindness and smiley "good mornings," are just flat out mean-spirited. There will always be a few people we have to walk away from or endure, recognizing that regardless of what we do, they will not respond in kind. It should not be our mission to conform them to our level of interpersonal grace. Just walk away. And put that business card in the x-file.

Jesus' teaching is clear on this subject. The Golden Rule's fundamental message lies in John 13:34–35: "A new command I give you: Love one another. As I have loved you, so you must love one another. By this all men will know that you are my disciples, if you love one another."

Not only are we commanded to love as Jesus loved, but we are told that our commitment to treating others well will show the world whose we are. Wouldn't it be great, daughter of the King, to love more of your marketplace sisters into the Kingdom based on your example of love and kindness?

RECAP

Integrity. A loaded word with plenty of implications and connotations and one lived out sometimes with lots of perspiration! It's not easy, in a world that so often accepts that which is not right, to always do the right thing—especially if no one is looking. However, a commitment to integrity in speech, image, and our modus operandi—how we do our work—will demonstrate our faith to our co-workers more fully than a thousand tracts or bumper stickers or the fish stuck on our computer monitor.

A commitment to integrity also allows us to approach our work and our career with the confidence that we are seeking God's path and His timing for what we do and how we do it in the marketplace. When we don't rush Him, when we let God be God and let Him give us the wisdom and strength to live out our calling, our faith doesn't falter in the workplace. In fact the opposite is true—it grows and intensifies, just like the integrity that He cultivates in our heart.

LESSONS AT WORK

Think:

• What area in this chapter is your challenging one? Is it speech? Image? Your MO?

• Have you ever been called into account for a breach in the integrity department? Why? What happened?

• What lessons have you learned in your own workplace regarding the essential need for integrity?

• Are there things that are acceptable in your business's culture that really aren't right for a believer to participate in?

• On the positive side: How have you demonstrated integrity in any of the areas we have discussed, and did you see the benefit from that?

Do:

• Find a copy of your company's values statement and see how it jives with your faith. Are your actions consistent? This isn't a time to evaluate everyone around you—just yourself! As a believer, can you kick it up a notch? Are there ways you can operate to demonstrate an even higher commitment to integrity and your company's values?

- Carefully observe your behavior during the next week. Identify some areas in which you can bump up your performance and therefore demonstrate a higher level of integrity. It may be something as simple as arriving a little early for your shift or leveling with your manager on where you *really* stand in completing that almost-due budget report.

- Discuss *talking* with another co-worker or friend in the business world whom you know wants to be pure in her speech. Develop a system with each other to avoid gossip and negative talk and to encourage one another to "love and good deeds" (Hebrews 10:24). Having some accountability is a great way to push integrity up to a new level.

- Start carefully proofreading your e-mails or presentations, if appropriate. If you are job-hunting, check your résumé one more time, ensuring it portrays the highest level of professionalism and an integrity-intense image.

CHAPTER SEVEN

The Significance of Work

LESSON #7
YOUR WORK IMPACTS
THE KINGDOM OF GOD.

"God is marshalling His people in the workplace as never before in history. God is up to something . . . ."
—Henry Blackaby

W e began this book with a bird's-eye view of our careers. We explored the fact that we must take ownership of our career development and growth, regardless of where we are in our season of work. We end this book at the 40,000-foot level too. Now we are going to venture into another realm of our life at work—the *significance* of what we do.

SIGNIFICANCE DEFINED

In this case, significance does not refer to what you do. In this chapter I do not define significance based on your job content, like whether you are developing a cure for cancer or teaching underachieving kids in a disadvantaged urban environment. Significance in our work is not dependent on whether we are nurses caring for preemies or CEOs running a nonprofit organization committed to rectifying one of our many social ills.

No, in this chapter, we will focus again on *how* we do what we do. The *how* of what we do can lend significance to those 40-some odd hours we spend each day in our vocation or avocation.

You are going to read stories of several women from across the spectrum of the work world, from one end of the country to another. Each of them has discovered an important fact of work life: Our marketplace can be our mission field, and we can have significant impact on the world around us regardless of position, title, or industry. Some of them have made tough choices when it came to place and/or position, then discovered greater satisfaction than they ever envisioned. Others have experienced a smooth and natural transition into what they do and where they do it, knowing all along they were moving in a direction that was both their desire and their calling.

Remember Karen Porter, the vice president we met from American Rice? She is passionate in her belief that we all can make a difference regardless of our position or company. "No matter what your position in the workplace, your niche is important to the overall well-being of the company," says Karen. "You make a difference when you do your job. And when you do it with excellence, you spread the joy of the Lord."

When it comes to having impact in our little corners of the world, we tend to think that some jobs are nobler than others. There has even been a bit of guilt-tripping in some circles that full-time ministry is really the best or only way to leave a mark for the Lord. Ed Silvoso, in his book *Anointed for Business*, writes, "The most common self-inflicted put down is 'I am not a pastor—I am just a layperson.' This is all part of a clever satanic scheme to neutralize apostles, prophets, evangelists, pastors and teachers along with the entire army of disciples already positioned in the workplace."

Does Mr. Silvoso's observation have an impact on you? Remember, "Our struggle is not against flesh and blood, but against the rulers, against the authorities, against the powers of this dark world and against the spiritual forces of evil in the heavenly realms" (Ephesians 6:12). When we believe that we cannot have significant impact in the marketplace where we spend the bulk of our days, we believe a lie from the enemy camp. When we convince ourselves that our sphere of influence is not big enough to make a difference, we have ceased to believe the Word that he is able "to do immeasurably more than all we ask or imagine, according to his power that is at work within us" (Ephesians 3:20).

WHEREVER YOU ARE

I believe this principle regarding the significance of our career applies regardless of where you are in your walk of work.

Settled into a comfortable routine and happy in your job? *Consider how you can kick it up a notch to not only grow professionally, but to serve faithfully as well.*

Hitting the pavement to find a new job or move within your current company? *Expand those prayers from, "Anything, Lord!" to "Where can You really use me, Lord?"*

Just starting out with a freshly printed diploma? *Dream big and recall God's promise to do immeasurably more than we can imagine within and through us. If you are still single, your potential for impact is, like, way big.*

Leaving college I was just excited about getting a job that was somewhat related to my degree and skills. I wouldn't say that I would have done just about *anything*, but almost! My second career position was for a nonprofit organization dedicated to drug abuse prevention—that was easy to get pretty jazzed about, realizing we were having a positive impact on kids and communities. When I first started at Dell, we were rallied around being the underdog scrapping for a spot on the high-tech map, and though it wasn't necessarily work with social impact, we still felt like we were part of something bigger and greater, albeit in a capitalistic sort of way.

As I have met more and more women in business, and as the company that I practically grew up in changed from the scrappy underdog to a global behemoth, my perspective on the significance of work has broadened.

Noted Christian leaders have commented in recent years that the greatest moves of ministry in this century will most likely occur in the marketplace. Perhaps most telling, some of the oldest and most venerated of Christian institutions, from the Billy Graham Training Center to Campus Crusade for Christ, have active and vibrant workplace-related ministries and events. The International Coalition of Workplace Ministries, for instance, exists to inspire, connect, and equip leaders who want to transform the workplace for Christ. Their Web site is a clearinghouse for information, resources, and organizations in the faith and work movement; the list is long and impressive.

WHEN WE BELIEVE THAT WE CANNOT HAVE SIGNIFICANT IMPACT IN THE MARKETPLACE WHERE WE SPEND THE BULK OF OUR DAYS, WE BELIEVE A LIE FROM THE ENEMY CAMP.

Deep in the heart of Texas, a retreat center called Laity Lodge is dedicated to help people who desire to know Christ, and what that means in the ordinary, everyday places and relationships of our lives. It is a place where, in a safe, quiet environment, the laity (from the Greek *laos*, "the people of God") can explore choices leading to growth—in creativity, effectiveness, and fulfillment. Many of their seminars and retreats are intended to encourage ordinary people to fulfill their call in the marketplace.

Space does not allow a listing of the myriad resources available today for equipping everyday people to do above-and-beyond-the-call work in their workplace. Clearly, this trend will not go away. The laity is well positioned to lead, and we ladies within that laity are just as qualified as anyone when the hand of God is moving us.

THE HAND THAT ROCKS THE CRADLE

We've often heard the expression: "The hand that rocks the cradle rules the world." So true. By raising godly children and managing godly homes, we women can exert mind-boggling influence. Fact is, these days many of us are often rocking a cradle then running off to a meeting. (There was a time when I would breast-feed, answer email, and sing a lullaby simultaneously. Talk about multitasking!)

Yes, along with this transformation in attitude about where ministry occurs, a transformation has come among women too. Consider the ministries of amazing women like Beth Moore and Joyce Meyer—two women with different styles but powerful teaching ministries. There are women in the marketplace too who have found their calling and are loving people into the Kingdom. The gals are coming out of the children's Sunday school closet and using skills they have learned in the marketplace to help build churches, run ministry fundraising campaigns, and serve in roles typically reserved for men in past generations.

Now before you get all fussy and start throwing felt story boards my way, please understand that I am not discounting those who love to teach in children's ministry. Just know that there are a lot of women like me who would rather give birth to a bowling ball than teach four-year-olds. And believe me—you would not *want* me teaching your four-year-old!

You would, however, want me to help with your church's internal communication program or marketing efforts for its building campaign. You would happily let me host a fund-raising dinner at my home for 50 potential donors to the new teen camping foundation. Women are beginning to learn that the God-given gifts they have and workplace competencies they have developed lend themselves to roles that look very different from the role of the ladies' quilting bee and Bible study circle of previous generations.

Now don't worry. I am perfectly happy embracing my femininity, and I long ago ditched my stuffy blue suits for a business wardrobe that looks quite ladylike. I do, however, believe strongly in equal work for equal pay. I believe we women can use our talents, skills, and God-given abilities both inside and outside the home.

The rest of this chapter will introduce you to some remarkable women who have done just that. Some of them are working today in cities across the country. Others hail from stories you heard in Sunday school— women who long ago went to their heavenly home but nonetheless had high-impact stories that are still told today. So, here we go—get ready to make some new friends.

WOMEN WHO ROCK—PART I

First, let's meet Lydia. We greet her in Acts 16. She is the first recorded convert to Christianity in Europe, and she and her whole household were baptized in Philippi.

Wow. A woman just might be credited with the establishment of the church in this chunk of the ancient world. Two things about her story are important to our study. One, she was a businesswoman: a dealer in purple cloth. Evidently her hometown of Thyatira was known for its brilliant purple dye.

Philippi was a colony of Rome and the leading city of the Macedonian district. It was a military outpost on the busy coast of the Aegean Sea. By the time Paul got there, the gold and silver mines operated by the Phoenicians years ago had been spent, but the city was still a hub of commercialization. Like all of the cities where Paul chose to preach, this one had strategic significance. Philippi is more than 250 miles from where Lydia was born, but perhaps she located her fabric selling business there because of the marketplace opportunities.

The second interesting thing about Lydia is that she was obviously not a wallflower. Paul uses an interesting word about her in his story. First of all, she made sure her whole household was baptized and then she flung wide the doors. Paul says "she persuaded us" to stay in her home while they were in town. Other translations use "constrained" and "prevailed upon us." Obviously, she had some power of influence not only over her household, which likely included some servants and maybe some of her employees, but also with Paul and his missionary companions. Later in the chapter, we see that Lydia opened her home to many of the Philippian believers during a difficult time of persecution (Acts 16:40).

Women play a predominant role in several other spots in the New Testament. In thirteen verses of personal greetings in Romans 16, nine of Paul's very personal messages are addressed to women.

The Old Testament shines light on some strong and powerful women that I love to read about over and over again. Deborah is one of my favorites. We meet her in Judges 4:4. She was the leader of Israel and a prophetess. Neither of those was a small job. This lady could multitask! The Israelites came to her to have their disputes settled. And as if this role was not important enough, she led the Israelites into a victorious battle over the Canaanites. Deborah must have been an impressive leader. When she called upon Barak to tell him that the Lord had commanded him to battle Sisera's Canaanite army, he said, "Okay, but I'm only going if you will go with me." I love what happens next. She says, "Very well" (I can hear her sigh), "I will go with you. But because of the way you are going about this, the honor will not be yours, for the Lord will hand Sisera over to a woman."

I am absolutely certain that this is the first time a collective, womanly shout was heard: "You go girl!"

Another interesting twist occurs later in this story of strong women. Sisera, the leader of this defeated army, gets away. He hides in the tent of Jael, a Kenite woman. He though he would be safe there because his clan was friendly with her clan.

Jael turns out to be a politician herself. She gives him a drink and agrees to let him hide. When he falls asleep exhausted from battle, she drives a tent peg into his head with a hammer. Whoa. We're talking PG-13 drama. This is another illustration of a woman willing to take the lead in a risky situation.

Deborah's story is concluded in Judges 5 with a song. Yes, one more example of this woman's many talents— settle disputes, lead an army, then break out into song. She and Barak sang a beautiful song of praise to the God who delivered them. It ends with the oft-quoted phrase: "So may all your enemies perish, oh Lord! But may they who love you be like the sun when it rises in its strength." Amen, sister.

I want to conclude our look at influential women of the ancient world by going back to the New Testament. I have been going to church all my life. That adds up to a lot of Easter Sunday sermons I've heard, but this year, perhaps because I was preparing to write this book, a blinding flash of the obvious hit me. Something I had read and heard preached many times but never really paid attention to: According to the gospels of Matthew, Mark, and John, the *women* were the first to see and speak with Jesus after His victory over death.

THE WOMEN WERE THE FIRST TO SEE AND SPEAK WITH JESUS AFTER HIS VICTORY OVER DEATH.

Here is what happens. Mary is standing outside the tomb weeping. Her world shattered three days earlier. She is the same woman from whom Jesus delivered seven demons. She literally owed her life to this teacher whom she had followed in earnest love and devotion, and now He was gone. Jesus' heart is so touched by her tears that He comes to her.

She's so distraught she doesn't recognize him when he speaks to her: "Woman, why are you crying?" "They have taken my Lord away," she mumbles through tears, "and I don't know where they have put Him." Finally Jesus says the one word He's said so many times in loving conversations with this faithful follower.

"Mary."

He speaks her name.

As Mary reaches out to touch Him, joyously crying *"Rabboni!"* He says, "Do not hold on to me, for I have not yet returned to the Father. Go instead to my brothers and tell them, 'I am returning to my Father and your Father, to my God and your God.'"

The headline news that the King of the Universe had overcome the powers of hell was entrusted to a woman. She had been delivered from a life of death and demonic pain. She was a simple woman who *didn't* deal in purple cloth or lead an army. We know little about her, but we do know enough to let her story soak us in the redeeming, releasing power of the Lord's love. We read enough about Mary Magdalene to see Jesus' respect for women and the role He wants us to play in the spreading of the Gospel. "Go tell those guys, Mary. Go tell them, and then you all get to work. I am alive!"

Wow. That blows me away.

The women of the Bible have remarkable stories, and the lives they led and lessons they left impact us today. For an even more in-depth exploration in the dynamic role of women in the world, read Ed Silvoso's book, *Women: God's Secret Weapon.*

There are also modern-day women who demonstrate to us the impact of women in the marketplace. And just as we saw in our Bible stories, they come from all walks of life. In our snippet of a Bible study we saw a businesswoman, a political leader, and a formerly demon-possessed woman. In the rest of this chapter you are going to meet a diverse group of modern-day women as well.

WOMEN WHO ROCK—PART II

In 2001, I quit working full time for the first time in my adult life. I was a little nervous. I thought I would have a lot of spare time on my hands and I would be tempted to sit on the couch, eat bonbons, and watch daytime TV all day. That turned out to be pretty far from the truth.

I had a new house to putter with, and my mom had just died, leaving some family business to attend to. Plus, our kids were as busy as anybody else's kids with school and friends and activities, and my husband was going through some big career-related decisions. I still haven't had time to eat a bonbon.

One thing I did, though, was get involved in a women's Bible study. Now I have to tell you, large groups of women make me nervous. I've always worked in industries and teams with mostly men. I'm a linear thinker, and although I love to shop and cook and do some other girly stuff, I don't like to talk on the phone or gab the day away. I'm not good at "small" talk. I was a little hesitant about getting into this big women's Bible study, although I really wanted to soak in the Word in a way I'd not had time to for years.

Dana Law was a breath of fresh air. She was my small group leader. She had wild red hair and a backpack that looked like a teddy bear. She followed all the rules but winked and looked the other way when we'd occasionally wander off on a non-sanctioned rabbit trail. I loved her. I also ate up the fabulous study of Moses and realized that I could survive being with big groups of women in broad daylight. The whole experience was an epiphany.

Dana was not just a great small group leader—she was a missionary. Back then, she worked in the photofinishing department of a large suburban grocery store, and she was always telling us about opportunities she'd had to share with co-workers or regular customers. I was amazed. While I'd taken advantage of some of the ministry opportunities God had placed in my path during my time in the workplace, my fear of what people would think led me to keep my mouth shut too many times.

Dana was fearless though. Her energy and enthusiasm for the Lord was contagious, and it was no wonder lives were changed in her wake. I want you to meet Dana and get a glimpse into her heart. See how God uses this woman whose pulpit is now the dining room of a local Chick-Fil-A—she's an associate there. She is proof positive that you don't have to have a fancy title or high falutin' job to have an impact for Christ.

DANA LAW, CHICK-FIL-A ASSOCIATE

My job is my mission field. I'm a working woman not because of the money, but because of the potential to share Jesus with others. I need the money, but I know God would supply my needs even if I didn't work. I have the ability, knowledge, and experience to work at a higher paying job with potential to have quite a career, but I choose to work in fast food because God led me there.

I prayed for a job where I could have a Christian boss and be used by God to share. My kids are all overseas, along with my grandkids, so I'm free to do this and focus on work because it is an excellent mission field. God said we are to tell others about Jesus. The Great Commission in Matthew 28:18 tells us, "All authority in heaven and on earth has been given to me. Therefore go and make disciples of all nations." I believe the best way to make disciples is by example.

I go to work each day not thinking about the work per se but how will I share Jesus. There are many hurting people out there. They need someone just to say, "I care, I love you and wow, Jesus really loves you! Let me tell you what He did." Sometimes you can only show that to people through your actions, but other times, God allows you time to tell them, too.

My daughter is a missionary overseas. We think the missionaries overseas have it hard, but I'm not sure. I've seen my daughter at work overseas, and even lived with her for a month. It is hard, but she doesn't have some of the same obstacles to overcome that we do here in the States! As a missionary at work in the U.S., I see firsthand the struggle we have with materialism. We have a car but we want a better one. We have clothes but we want better ones. The list goes on.

As a working woman who is missions-oriented, I have to go to work with a desire to do my best for God and focus on Him. If I do more than my fair share at work, it is not about getting ahead, it is about serving God. Being like Christ in the workplace is about having a servant heart. Jesus served. He was never too tired, too busy, or too high and mighty. He was humble enough to do any type of job or deal with any type of people. God uses me, just a woman working in fast food. I know that as small as it seems to me, my job is great to God. So, wow! I have a mission! When He comes to get me and I see Jesus face to face, I can meet Him with eager anticipation and the expectation of hearing, "Well done my good and faithful child. You got up and went out, even though you didn't have to."

Work can be your mission field. I can so see God smiling, telling the angels, "Look! See! That's My child going out. That's My obedient child!" As parents, we know how it feels when our kids get a job and do it well. Our heavenly Father is just excited when we are obedient and go to work and do it well.

Just a woman working in fast food, indeed! She is not focusing on making a living, but she is completely focusing on helping others find life.

Did you like her story? Well there are more. In the process of writing this book, God placed remarkable women in my path, both from my current circle and new friends who have amazing stories of faith at work and careers of significance.

Remember the great debate we discussed at the beginning of the chapter? Full-time ministry or secular work? Which counts more? Well, the next story will broaden your perspective on that issue. Meet my new friend from Illinois, Sharon Swing.

SHARON SWING, ILLUMAX PARTNERS AND SWING CONSULTING

I grew up thinking God was a cosmic line judge who would tell me when I was in and out of bounds. Not the kind of God you would want to get to know. I went to college and never even thought about finding a church, not because I was rebellious but more because I thought church was irrelevant to my life.

As I started my career, I climbed the corporate ladder and had everything I thought would make me happy. But I wasn't. One day I challenged God, "If You are real, You have to be bigger than I grew up believing You to be!" Two weeks later, at a workplace ministry event, He proved it. At 28 I had an experience where I realized that my attempts to control my own life were worthless. Some people give their lives to God—I threw mine at Him and begged Him to make something of it.

Over time, I found out that God had a much better plan and that plan could be an adventure that I could have never imagined myself. Because God loves me, He sees what I can become and leads me in ways that help me to become what He intends. I believe that God wants all of me—all the time. No Sunday spirituality that gets put on the sideline the rest of the week. And what that means is that my work matters intensely to God.

When I was employed in the marketplace in a corporate job, I asked God to make me an instrument of His peace so that others would see Him in the work I did. I had a position of influence in a Fortune 500 company. Much to my delight, God arranged circumstances where people would ask me questions about my faith. On one occasion after a long week of hard work in Colorado with a team of people I led, we went on a weekend ski trip.

We sat down to dinner one night and someone said, "This feels like family. Someone should pray." They all looked at me since I was the only one known to be spiritual in the group. That started a four-hour long conversation about Christianity. One man in particular was very curious. I followed up by sending him a Bible and Bill Hybel's Christianity 101 tape series. After six weeks, he called me and said, "I read that; now what?" We invited him and his wife to church for Christmas

Eve services. His wife, after being a religious church-attender for most of her life, began a relationship with Jesus that night. Since then, they have been involved in leading small groups for seekers and have introduced many people to their Friend and Savior, Jesus.

When I started my own organizational development consulting practice in 1991, I knew the business belonged to God. I asked Him to lead me to the work that would use my gifts to His glory, and help me to grow and learn. I asked that God would allow me to work with people who didn't know Him, and that I might have the opportunity to introduce people to Jesus.

My first client, twelve years ago, was an atheist. He told me, "I respect you. I think you are smart. But you are a Christian. I don't get it!" Over time, this man has called me on several occasions for very personal reasons, when he is at a spiritual crossroads. I am currently doing consulting work with the company he works for, through his referral, and he has hired me as his personal coach. He says, "I'm at a crossroads in my life, and I'm fogged in." This atheist has hired a Christian to help him plan his life and find what he's missing. Coincidence? I think not.

Some people see their work as the plot of the story, and the relationships as the subplot. I like to think that the relationships I build are the plot, and the work itself is the subplot of the adventure. Throughout the past twelve years, God has honored my prayer to use my work to put me in places where people need Jesus. In fact, I think He strategically places and "calls" Christians to be in the workplace to love people into a relationship with Him.

With each strategic plan I help to create, I ask for God's wisdom. Each meeting I facilitate, I try to listen intently and value each person, regardless of his or her position in the company, just as God does. I know that the quality of my work just gets me into the game. If clients respect my work, maybe they'll ask about something that will allow me to give a reason for why I do things the way I do—and be able to share a bit about my leader and friend, Jesus.

Most of all, I know that God has used my work as a way to change me and grow me. God gives me enough success that I can give Him credit for it, yet humbles me often enough to keep me focused on what He wants to accomplish in me. Oswald Chambers said, "God engineers our circumstances so that we will trust Him." I want to grow in trusting God to supply the next client, to give me wisdom for my client's business and life, and for God to grant enough self-awareness so I don't miss what He is trying to teach me. Since He's the God of the universe, why wouldn't I want His involvement in every detail of my work?

Sharon's career path has taken her from the corporate and consulting marketplace to ministry and back again to consulting. As you read her words, you could tell that she believes strongly that her work has significance and that God uses her wherever He has her—inside or outside the walls of a church or faith-based organization. Now meet Mary, another woman with corporate experience who now does the self-employment dance. Here is her story.

MARY PARTRIDGE, IMPACT CONSULTING

My mom was a career woman—working for my deaf father, who was an independent CPA. That meant many long hours away from us kids during tax season and a few other times of the year, but there was never a question in my mind that she loved us and that we were a priority. My grandmother lived with us, so we had an instant "nanny"—but with the added feature of a grandmother's love! Mom would tell us about meeting with judges, IRS agents, and others, and how she had managed the conversations and situations. Meanwhile, one of my cousins became widowed and found a job as a receptionist—a job she kept until she retired, because she had no other skills. So, between those two role models, I think I decided very early on that (1) I'd have a career; (2) it was possible to raise kids who were secure in my love even if I worked, and (3) I needed to "stay in school" to acquire skills that would allow me to have any job I wanted.

So, as I got my MBA, and later worked for a Fortune 100 company, I was comfortable talking with the CEO and working with senior leaders, because in my frame of reference, women did that sort of thing. After nine years with the corporation, I learned that my dad (who lived in another state) was quite ill. I would soon have three weeks' vacation, but didn't know how that would be spread out to cover time with my parents, time with my in-laws, vacations with kids, and alone time with my hubby.

I made the difficult decision to leave the fast-track career I had worked hard to fit into, and begin consulting so that I would have more flexibility. That decision proved to make me ever-mindful of the difficulty of making choices in line with your priorities. It has meant no benefits, wild fluctuations in cash flow—some down cycles lasting for years—and the challenge to continue my self-development while producing results.

It also meant that I was able to be with my dad many times when he was critically ill, and many times when he was well enough to enjoy the fellowship with my husband, my children, and me. I had no regrets when he passed away, because I had made him a priority in my life.

Since that time, I've had the flexibility to sit with a friend in the hospital for a week before her son passed away, take an annual trip with my mother and my sister, and do many other important things that I could not have done if I had been on a corporate payroll. I once thought I might be called to full-time ministry, but I have seen how God has allowed me to be "full time" in ministry while having a career—by having time for friends in need, actively loving my family, or serving in my community and church.

I do not look back on my corporate experience with any negative feelings at all. That experience helped prepare me to do what I do now—it was essential! I loved it while I was there, and I love what I do now. God just placed me in a different situation, and I thank Him for giving me the free time I've had for family, friends, and volunteer activities since being self-employed. I can see Him bringing it all together. For example, I've started doing some "billable" work for nonprofits, using my depth of experience as a volunteer. I never considered that the volunteer work would lead to income. But, right when I needed it, He provided. He is indeed the Master Weaver!

Mary's story reveals once again that God provides for us throughout our careers, even when we make tough choices and take giant risks. As a leadership development expert, she has the opportunity to impact people in a professional sense. As a self-employed businesswoman, she has the opportunity to affect her friends, church, and community, and share her faith. Now meet another friend of mine who has seen life-altering career path changes and the hand of a loving God in her life. Meet Cici Meyer.

CICI MEYER, PRIORITY ASSOCIATES

When I was a kid I decided I wanted to be an international banker. I didn't even know what that meant, but it sounded like I'd make a lot of money and get to travel! I was always very driven and very successful at whatever I did, so I chose finance when I enrolled in college and set my sights on a management position as soon as I graduated.

I went to work for Andersen Consulting. I liked the fact that their management consulting track was based on merit and performance, and I figured I could outperform anybody. I set very high goals for myself both professionally and financially and I achieved them, but I was not happy.

I was baffled. I was so goal-oriented and I was hitting on all cylinders. Why wasn't this satisfying? A boyfriend at the time even asked me, "Are you ever going to be satisfied?" On the outside, I reacted defensively, "Well, of course!" but on the inside I was really beginning to wonder.

I did not grow up in a Christian home and always thought church was irrelevant to my life. In fact, I wouldn't want to have associated with most of the Christians I knew at the time.

I got involved with a guy at work and the relationship went south. It was awful but I tried to act like everything was okay. Around that time, a friend at work invited me to church. To this day, I still don't know why I agreed to go. My sister, who'd become a Christian, was also after me. "The only person who will never let you down is Jesus," she kept telling me.

Well, finally, at the age of 27, the gospel hit me for the first time. The friend who invited me to church moved away but I kept going. I got involved with church and with Priority

Associates, the workplace ministry of Campus Crusade for Christ. That helped me connect the dots between my spiritual life and my work. I really began to pursue the Spirit-filled life and I knew God was changing me because I used to cuss like a sailor and God completely took that habit away!

At the same time, though, I was working like crazy. I was traveling all over the place and I'd been at that company for ten years. I had my sights set on making partner—that had always been my goal. But then I looked at some of the folks at that level and their lives were a wreck. I couldn't imagine what I should do. I began praying that I could take a leave of absence.

My company offered me an eight-month sabbatical. While I was off, I called my friend at Priority Associates and asked if I could hang out with her. I wanted to be able to share my faith but was scared to do it. I began going on appointments with her, and God helped me develop the skills and tools to share how Jesus changed my life.

It was then that my career began to take a huge turn and I felt led to join the ministry of Priority Associates. I had no idea what I would do there. I asked the staff if they could use some-one with my skills—project management, strategic analysis and planning, presentations—the answer was a resounding yes. So I made the leap from the corporate ladder to ministry.

When I began raising support, I went back and visited with some friends at work. I was shocked—and a bit disap-pointed—to learn how many of my former colleagues were Christians. Several people said to me, "Cici, I wanted so badly to talk to you about God, but I was afraid you wouldn't listen." How many people are there out there like me, who wanted to hear, but no one would tell them?

I am so glad God led me this direction. I still use my cor-porate competencies, but for a higher calling now. We help people in the workplace connect faith to the rest of life and help young professionals see the difference that living an integrated life makes. I still do things that count in the workplace—like transformational leadership training—but there's a more important underlying cause to what I do. I am all about developing people now, from the inside out.

Cici's story is not unlike many other professional women who have discovered that significance lies not necessarily in what they do but how they do it and who they do it for. She could easily transition back to a consulting job in the marketplace if she wanted and her skills would still be used. The competency that she has developed, to share her faith in a way that is relevant to young professionals, will count for eternity regardless of where Cici does her job.

The last person I want you to meet has taken a ministry/business track combining a higher motive with a profit motive. Her story shows us that we can sometimes unite faith and business in a way that uses our skills and reaches people with good news at the same time. Meet Kathleen Jackson, publisher of *The Godly Business Woman Magazine*.

KATHLEEN JACKSON, PUBLISHER

I had a high-level management job in a demanding corporation. I worked for a tough boss, had a daily three-hour commute and a crazy schedule. I was making more money than I had ever made in my life but, in spite of that, my husband asked me to quit my job.

I immediately became defensive. There was no way. But then he starting mimicking me on my cell phone, issuing orders and fussing about the things not getting taken care of around the house while I was so busy working. I was shocked. For weeks I battled my pride, but then submitted. There was no use arguing with God or my husband. This was what I was supposed to do.

For years we had felt God leading us to publish a magazine. I had my eye on something real estate related—something with significant income potential. But my husband had another idea. He thought we should do something to deal with the tough issues working women face in the corporate world.

I entered into a season of prayer like no other. I did my homework and researched all the Christian publications I could get my hands on. I also sought godly counsel from Bill and Vonette Bright, co-founders of Campus Crusade for Christ, and my pastor. *The Godly Business Woman* magazine was born in 1988 as a result of my husband's leading and a lot of prayer. Today it has transformed into an online presence with a global reach—literally connecting working women around the globe!

My goal with the magazine is to encourage women, especially single working moms. In addition to publishing the magazine, I also have the opportunity to speak throughout the country about my experiences. Over the years of my professional life, God was training and preparing me to be able to publish a magazine. The skills I gained in the 26 years I spent in training, development, and marketing in corporate America have definitely paid off and I use those skills now in my publishing business.

It is a business. We have to make a profit. We want to expand and grow, but we are about a bigger mission. It was not easy to set aside my pride and make this move, but there is no doubt that God led me this direction. Sometimes it is tough, but in the process of making the transition, every time

I prayed about it, I felt more peace. God directed me to all the appropriate people for counsel and advice and helped me to make the decision that yes—I can do this for Him. "I can do everything through him who gives me strength" (Philippians 4:13).

Well, there you have it from four new friends.

- A fast-food server with a heart bursting with passion for God
- A consultant who has let God lead her back and forth across the marketplace/ministry divide
- A driven young woman whose ambitious heart led her out of the corporate world into full-time ministry
- A self-employed businesswoman who has faced tough choices and ups and downs with faith-filled grace
- A seasoned executive whose husband and faithful God led her to launch a ministry-based business

What we learn from these women, and the countless others out there like them, is that God uses us mightily when we are open to be used by Him. Sometimes that openness to God's call must be fortified with a high degree of courage and maturity we might not think we possess.

BE BRAVE AND SHINE!

One of my favorite Old Testament stories is that of Gideon. I think I will probably use his illustration of latent bravery in every book I ever write. We meet him in Judges 6–8. I encourage you to read the story for yourself, but here's my condensed version of it.

The Israelites are scared to death of the Midianites. They are hiding and shaking in their boots. Gideon is among the knock-kneed. He's hiding in a wine press to sift wheat to keep it from the Midianites. Not only were these people fearful for their lives, they were intent on protecting their food supply. (I can relate to that!)

Now get this picture. The ancient wine press was not necessarily huge. He probably had to crouch down so as to not be seen. All of a sudden, an angel shows up. Talk about having your cover blown. These guys were not nondescript angels; in fact, most of the time when they appear to people in the Bible, the mortals drop to the ground in fear and awe.

This angel utters words that must have sounded hilarious to Gideon, "The Lord is with you, mighty warrior." Gideon's initial response is also typical of our response to God: "Who me? You talkin' to me?" Gideon is hiding from an enemy that God is ready to defeat. God just needs leaders to take the army out into battle. Yes, women, God is talking to us too. The Lord used shaky ol' Gideon, and an army he pared down to a mere 300, to overthrow a country. He can use us in our workplaces too.

We may not feel like mighty warriors. We may feel ill equipped and outnumbered like Gideon, but we can do battle against the spirits of sadness and hopelessness and loneliness that wreak havoc in the lives of our co-workers. We can do that battle, regardless of our jobs, and have significant impact on the people around us.

Ed Silvoso likes Gideon too. He mentions his story in the book, *Anointed for Business*. I really like what Ed writes and the challenge he presents to all of us in the marketplace today: "Obedience in spite of fear is what makes Gideon such a hero."

Those women you met earlier are ordinary women like you. They have fears and doubts just like the rest of us. Sure, some of them have more training than others, they have different gifts and skills and abilities, but regardless of all that we *all* have the same calling:

> "You are the light of the world. A city on a hill cannot be hidden. Neither do people light a lamp and put it under a bowl. Instead they put it on its stand, and it gives light to everyone in the house. In the same way, let your light shine before men, that they may see your good deeds and praise your Father in heaven." (Matthew 5:14–16)

Your hill may be the corporate boardroom or the basement of a warehouse. Your lampstand may sport a vice-president title or a simple plastic name badge that reads "Bill's Grill" with your name scrawled on it in smudged ink. You may work full time or part time, love your job or really wish you had a new one. You might wish you could quit altogether or dream that there were more hours in the day because you enjoy your vocation so much.

Wherever you are on that career continuum, you are called to be brave and to shine. Not to beat people over the head with your Bible and drag them kicking and screaming to church, but to love on them long enough that the rough edges come off and they ask you, "Why are you the way you are? What is so different about you?"

"Well, let's go to lunch and let me tell you about the hope that is within me." Gulp. To even say those words may scare you, but be brave and shine anyway. On our own, we can't do much of anything, but as Philippians says, "I can do everything through him who gives me strength."

PARTING THOUGHTS

Life is a faith-walk and usually not a cakewalk. As I conclude this book, I wonder about my future. I am stunned by the turns my career has taken, the fact that a year ago I only dreamed of being a published author and now I've spent the better part of six months writing not one, but two books. (My other book is titled *Slow Dancing on Death's Door.*)

I don't have a clue whether my books will perform. They may be my first two books, but they might be my last two as well! It's a faith walk for me too, friend.

Given that, I could easily dust off my résumé, polish it up with the cool consulting gigs I've done in the past four years, and hoof it back into corporate America—get a "real" job. But instead, I'm practicing what I am preaching. I'm moving my career forward in faith and, with God's help, being brave. In the process I hope to shine a message of hope and redemption and higher calling to women across our country, across the broad spectrum of what it looks like to be employed today.

I'll goof up periodically, I'm sure. I'll say something I shouldn't or make a really dumb decision I will regret later. But that's the great thing about your ultimate boss being God. His performance management system is all about grace: getting up, dusting off, and starting over.

My job title may change again a hundred times between now and the day I finally hang up my keyboard, turn in my cell phone, and permanently trade my high heels for flip flops. Regardless of what I do, where God calls me, I will know that because of what His Word says, I am set apart for greatness in Him. My worth is not defined by my career. My impact is measured not in how many cool jobs I have or books I sell or audiences I speak to, but in how I have demonstrated God's immeasurable love for people.

As we conclude, I encourage you to memorize a Bible verse. Carry it in your purse or briefcase. Stick it on your cubicle wall. "'I know the plans I have for you,' declares the Lord, 'plans to prosper you and not to harm you, plans to give you a hope and a future'" (Jeremiah 29:11).

Our careers may take turns we never imagined. Our jobs may veer in directions that break our hearts or thrill our souls. We may willingly jump on and off the fast track throughout our career or choose to never leap on that track to begin with. Regardless, as working women, we *can* be successful when we remember the supreme and loving architect of who we are and what we are to become. *Daughter of the King.* Now *that's* a fabulous title for a business card.

New Hope® Publishers is a division of WMU®, an international organization that challenges Christian believers to understand and be radically involved in God's mission. For more information about WMU, go to www.wmu.com. More information about New Hope books may be found at www.newhopepublishers.com. New Hope books may be purchased at your local bookstore.